CHURCH LAW & TAX REPORT

The 2006 Compensation Handbook for Church Staff

James F. Cobble, Jr., D.Min., Ed.D. & Richard R. Hammar, J.D., LL.M., CPA

Christian Ministry Resources

617 Greenbrook Pkwy

Matthews, NC 28104

www.churchlawtoday.com

This publication is designed to provide accurate and authoritative information in regard to the subject matter covered. It is sold with the understanding that the publisher is not engaged in rendering legal, accounting, or other professional service. If legal advice or other expert assistance is required, the services of a competent professional person should be sought. "From a Declaration of Principles jointly adopted by a Committee of the American Bar Association and a Committee of Publishers and Associations."

Table of Contents

Chapter 1

Introduction

Welcome to _The 2006 Compensation Handbook for Church Staff_. Please take a few minutes to read this introduction. It provides several ways to maximize your use of this book.

The _Compensation Handbook_ was developed to provide church leaders and employees with a current and reliable picture of compensation practices across a broad spectrum of American churches. It presents survey data from nearly 2,800 churches representing approximately 6,650 staff members. The survey data was obtained between January 2005 and May 2004 from churches that subscribe to _Church Law & Tax Report_, _Church Treasurer Alert!_, or _Church Secretary Today_. This information can play an important role in determining equitable compensation packages for church staff members. The _Compensation Handbook_ can help you:

- to determine appropriate compensation levels for nine key pastoral, professional, and support staff positions.

- to develop effective compensation packages—guidelines are given to maximize net income while remaining in compliance with federal tax laws.

- to provide church workers with a statistical framework for evaluating their present compensation package—comparisons can be made regarding church size, budget, setting, and other important variables.

- to develop an objective standard for evaluating requests for raises and changes in benefits.

- to assist denominational offices and other ecclesiastical organizations in promoting equitable and fair compensation practices within their churches.

- to better understand the nature of church compensation planning.

How To Make The Best Use Of This Book

Anyone engaged in compensation planning for church staff members should first become familiar with some basic federal tax laws. How a compensation package is structured can either help or hurt a church staff member. Chapter 2 provides a detailed discussion of the major tax laws that affect the compensation of church staff, and provides tax saving tips.

Chapter 3 provides guidance on reading and using the data found in the tables throughout this book. Included is an example that illustrates how to determine compensation ranges for a senior pastor. The same process can be used for all staff positions.

Chapter 4 provides comparisons between the national averages of the nine staff positions included in this study. The chapter begins by providing an employment profile for each staff position. Table 4-3 provides a comparative ranking of each position along with the standard deviation for each national average. Standard deviation is an important statistical calculation that is explained in both chapters 3 and 4. Denominational comparisons are also presented in this chapter.

Chapters 5-13 provide detailed information on each individual staff position. Natural curiosity will pull most church staff members immediately to the chapter which presents data about their position. Remember, though, understanding chapters 2 and 3 is critical to using this book in an effective manner.

Finally, chapter 14 provides a statistical abstract of the churches participating in this study. A graphical representation of the data is found in the appendices.

Data Analysis

Inconclusive or faulty survey data were not included in the survey. Figures that appeared unrealistic or way outside the normal distribution were eliminated to avoid skewing the results. These results represent the churches that participated in the survey. The sampling population used was a fair representation of American churches, but certain church sizes, budget sizes, and denominations have a stronger representation than others. To the extent possible, we have attempted to organize the data in ways that avoid small samples. At times, however, small samples simply reflect a reality such as rural churches with an attendance over 1,000, or churches smaller than 100 with a full-time business administrator. Nevertheless, sample size should be taken into account when considering the value of any particular finding. Standard deviations were calculated for the average compensation of each position. Some variables, however, reflected more of a linear relationship with compensation than did others. That relationship also changed from one position to another. The Pearson product-moment correlation coefficient was calculated to determine the strength of relationship between compensation and church size, and compensation and church budget for each of the nine positions. Coefficients of determination and nondetermination were also calculated to gain a better intuitive notion of the strength of the relationships between size and compensation, and budget and compensation. While this study does not make explicit reference to those findings, they do provide the basis for the inferences made at various points within the text about correlations.

Chapter 2

Compensation Planning

Synopsis. Compensation planning for clergy and other church staff presents several unique issues that are not well understood by many church leaders and their advisers. This chapter clears away the confusion and presents 19 key considerations to review while doing compensation planning.

Most churches will adopt year 2006 compensation packages for their ministers and lay staff members in the final months of 2005. Now is a good time to review several possible components of a compensation package. Consider the following.

1. Salary. The most basic component of church staff compensation is salary. There are two important considerations to keep in mind with respect to staff salaries—the amount of the salary, and the use of "salary reduction agreements." These two issues will be discussed separately.

a. Amount. Staff salaries ordinarily are set by the church board. Churches generally may pay any amount they wish, with one very big exception—if a church pays unreasonably high compensation to a pastor or other employee there are two possible consequences:

(1) Loss of tax-exempt status. In order for a church or any other charity to maintain its tax-exempt status it must meet a number of conditions. One condition is that it cannot pay unreasonably high compensation to any person. There are two considerations to note. First, very few charities have lost their exempt status for paying unreasonable compensation. The IRS has been very reluctant to impose this remedy. Few if any legitimate churches have lost their exempt status on this ground. Second, the law does not define what amount of compensation is unreasonable, and neither the IRS nor the courts have provided much clarification.

> ☞ **Example.** One federal appeals court concluded that combined annual income of $115,680 paid by a religious organization to its founder and his wife was *not* excessive.

> ☞ **Example.** The court in the "PTL" bankruptcy case concluded that maximum reasonable compensation for Jim Bakker would have been $133,100 in 1984, $146,410 in 1985, $161,051 in 1986, and $177,156 in 1987. The court based its conclusions on a comparison of the salaries of other nonprofit officers in the state.

(2) Intermediate sanctions. The IRS can assess "intermediate sanctions" against employees of churches and other charities who are paid "excess benefits" (defined as unreasonable compensation). Note that the IRS still can revoke the exempt status of any charity that pays excessive compensation to an employee. However, it is now more likely that excessive compensation will result in intermediate sanctions rather than loss of exempt status. To illustrate, why should a major university lose its tax-exempt status because it pays excessive compensation to its football coach?

It is very important for church leaders to be familiar with intermediate sanctions, since the law allows the IRS to assess large penalties against both highly compensated persons and members of a governing board who authorized the excessive compensation. The intermediate sanctions the IRS can impose include the following:

- *Tax on disqualified persons.* A "disqualified person" (someone, like a senior pastor, with significant administrative responsibilities) who benefits from an excess benefit transaction is subject to an excise tax equal to 25 percent of the amount of the "excess benefit" (the amount by which actual compensation exceeds the fair market value of services rendered). This tax is assessed against the disqualified person directly, not his or her employer.

- *Additional tax on disqualified persons.* If a disqualified person fails to "correct" the excess benefit by the time the IRS assesses the 25 percent tax, then the IRS can assess an additional tax of 200 percent of the excess benefit. The law specifies that a disqualified person can "correct" the excess benefit transaction by "undoing the excess benefit to the extent possible, and taking any additional measures necessary to place the organization in a financial position not worse than that in which it would be if the disqualified person were dealing under the highest fiduciary standards."

- *Tax on organization managers.* If the IRS assesses the 25 percent tax against a disqualified person, it is permitted to impose an additional 10 percent tax (up to a maximum of $10,000) on any "organization manager" who participates in an excess benefit transaction knowing it is such a transaction, unless the manager's participation "is not willful and is due to reasonable cause." A "manager" is an officer, director, or trustee. IRS regulations clarify that the managers collectively cannot be liable for more than $10,000 for any one transaction.

> ⊃ **Key point.** The intermediate sanctions law imposes an excise tax on members of a church's governing board who vote for a compensation package that the IRS determines to be excessive. This makes it essential for board members to carefully review the reasonableness of compensation packages.

Charities, disqualified persons, and governing boards may rely on a "presumption of reasonableness" with respect to a compensation arrangement if it was approved by a board of directors (or committee of the board) that: (1) was composed entirely of individuals unrelated to and not subject to the control of the disqualified person involved in the arrangement; (2) obtained and relied upon objective "comparability" information, such as (a) compensation paid by similar organizations, both taxable and tax-exempt, for comparable positions, (b) independent compensation surveys by nationally recognized independent firms, or (c) actual written offers from similar institutions competing for the services of the disqualified person; and (3) adequately documented the basis for its decision.

> ⊃ **Key point.** The law creates a presumption that a minister's compensation package is reasonable if approved by a church board that relied upon objective "comparability" information, including independent compensation surveys by nationally recognized independent firms. One of the more comprehensive compensation surveys for church workers is this text. This means that most ministers will be able to use this text to establish the presumption of reasonableness. But it also suggests that the IRS will rely on the data in this text in any attempt to impose intermediate sanctions against ministers.

IRS regulations clarify that "revenue based pay" arrangements in which an employee's compensation is based on a percentage of the employer's total revenues do not automatically result in an excess benefit transaction triggering intermediate sanctions. Rather, "all relevant facts and circumstances" must be considered.

▲ **Caution.** In a series of four rulings published in 2004 the IRS for the first time assessed intermediate sanctions against a pastor as a result of excess benefits paid to him (and members of his family) by his church. Intermediate sanctions are substantial excise taxes the IRS can impose on persons who receive excess benefits from a tax-exempt organization. The IRS concluded that a pastor's personal use of church property (vehicles, cell phones, credit cards, etc.) and nonaccountable reimbursements (not supported by adequate documentation of business purpose) that a church pays its pastor, are "automatic excess benefits" resulting in intermediate sanctions, regardless of the amount involved, unless they are reported as taxable income by the church on the pastor's W-2, or by the pastor on Form 1040, for the year in which the benefits are provided. This is a stunning interpretation of the tax code and regulations that will directly affect the compensation practices of many churches, and expose some church staff members to intermediate sanctions.

⊃ **Recommendation.** Churches that pay a minister (or any staff member) more than two standard deviations above the national average for comparable positions should obtain a legal opinion from an experienced tax attorney confirming that the amount paid is not "unreasonable" and will not expose the employee or the board to intermediate sanctions. See chapter 4 for a discussion of standard deviations.

✎ **Tax savings tip.** Ministers and other church staff members should carefully review their W-2 or 1099 to be sure that it does not report more income than was actually received. If an error was made, the church should issue a corrected tax form (Form W-2c for an employee, or a "corrected" Form 1099 for a self-employed worker).

b. Salary reduction agreements. Many churches have established "salary reduction agreements" to handle certain staff expenses. The objective is to reduce a worker's taxable income, since only the income remaining after the various "reductions" is reported on the worker's W-2 or 1099 form at the end of the year. It is important for churches to understand that they cannot reduce a worker's taxable income through salary reductions unless specifically allowed by law.

Here are three ways that taxable income can be reduced through salary reduction agreements:

(1) *Tax-sheltered annuity contributions.* Salary reduction agreements can be used to contribute to a tax-sheltered annuity (sometimes called a "403(b) annuity), if the salary reductions meet certain conditions.

(2) *"Cafeteria plans."* Salary reduction agreements also can be used to fund "cafeteria plans" (including "flexible spending arrangements") if several conditions are met. A cafeteria plan is a written plan established by an employer that allows employees to choose between cash and a "menu" of nontaxable benefits specified by law (including employer-provided medical insurance premiums, group-term life insurance, and dependent care).

(3) *Housing allowances.* A church can designate a portion of a minister's salary as a housing allowance, and the amount so designated is not subject to income tax if certain conditions are met. Housing allowances are addressed later in this chapter.

⊃ **Observation.** In most cases, "salary reductions" will not accomplish the goal of reducing a minister's taxable income. The income tax regulations prohibit the widespread practice of funding "accountable" reimbursement arrangements through salary reductions. This topic is addressed later in this chapter.

2. Housing allowances. The most important tax benefit available to ministers who own or rent their homes is the housing allowance. Ministers who own their home do not pay federal income taxes on the amount of their compensation that their employing church designates in advance as a housing allowance, to the extent that the allowance represents compensation for ministerial services, is used to pay housing expenses, and does not exceed the annual fair rental value of the home (furnished, plus utilities). Housing-related expenses include rent, mortgage payments, utilities, repairs, furnishings, insurance, property taxes, additions, and maintenance. Ministers who rent a home or apartment do not pay federal income taxes on the amount of their compensation that their employing church designates in advance as a housing allowance to the extent that the allowance represents compensation for ministerial services and is used to pay rental expenses such as rent, furnishings, utilities, and insurance. Unfortunately, many churches fail to designate a portion of a minister's compensation as a housing allowance. This deprives their minister of an important tax benefit.

Ministers who live in a church-owned parsonage that is provided "rent-free" as compensation for ministerial services do not include the annual fair rental value of the parsonage as income in computing their federal income taxes. The annual fair rental value is not "deducted" from the minister's income. Rather, it is not reported as additional income anywhere on Form 1040 (as it generally would be by non-clergy workers). Ministers who live in a church-provided parsonage do not pay federal income taxes on the amount of their compensation that their employing church designates in advance as a parsonage allowance, to the extent that the allowance represents compensation for ministerial services and is used to pay parsonage-related expenses such as utilities, repairs, and furnishings.

> ✎ **Tax savings tip.** Ministers who live in church parsonages, and who incur any out-of-pocket expenses in maintaining the parsonage (such as utilities, property taxes, insurance, furnishings, or lawn care) should be sure that their employing church designates in advance a portion of their annual compensation as a "parsonage allowance". Such an allowance is not included on the minister's W-2 or 1099 at the end of the year and is nontaxable in computing federal income taxes to the extent the minister incurs housing expenses of at least that amount. This is a very important tax benefit for ministers living in church-provided parsonages. Unfortunately, many ministers and church boards are not aware of this benefit, or are not taking advantage of it.

Note that these exclusions are for federal income tax purposes only. Ministers cannot exclude the fair rental value of a parsonage or a housing allowance when computing their self-employment (Social Security) taxes.

> ⊃ **Recommendation.** Ministers should be sure that the designation of a housing or parsonage allowance for year 2006 is on the agenda of the church board for one of its final meetings in 2005. The designation should be an official action of the board or congregation, and it should be duly recorded in the minutes of the meeting. The IRS also recognizes designations included in employment contracts and budget line items—assuming in each case that the designation was duly adopted by the church board (or the congregation in a business meeting).

How much should a church board or congregation designate as a housing allowance? Many churches base the allowance on their minister's estimate of actual housing expenses for the new year. The church provides the minister with a form on which anticipated housing expenses for the new year are reported. For ministers who own their homes, the form asks for projected expenses in the following categories: down payment, mortgage payments, property taxes, property insurance, utilities, furnishings and appliances, repairs and improvements, maintenance, and miscellaneous. Many churches designate an allowance in excess of the anticipated expenses itemized by the minister. Basing the allowance solely on a minister's actual expenses will penalize the minister if housing expenses in fact turn out to be higher than expected. In other words, the allowance should take into account unexpected housing costs or inaccurate projections of expenses.

⊃ **Recommendation.** Plan a mid-year review of the housing allowance to make sure that the designated amount is sufficient to cover actual expenses.

⊃ **Observation.** The compensation survey summarized over the next several chapters reveals that housing allowances are claimed by several associate ministers, administrators, music directors, secretaries, and custodians. However, it is important to note that the housing allowance is available only if two conditions are met: (1) the recipient is a minister, and (2) the allowance is provided as compensation for services performed in the exercise of ministry. In many cases, these conditions will not be satisfied by administrators, music directors, secretaries, and custodians. See chapter 3 of Richard Hammar's annual *Church and Clergy Tax Guide* (available from the publisher of this text) for more information.

3. Equity allowances. Ministers who live in church-owned parsonages are denied one very important benefit of home ownership—the opportunity to accumulate "equity" in a home over the course of many years. Many ministers who have lived in parsonages during much of their active ministry often face retirement without housing. Their fellow ministers who purchased a home early in their ministry often can look forward to retirement with a home that is either substantially or completely debt-free. To avoid the potential hardship often suffered by a minister who lives in a parsonage, some churches increase their minister's compensation by an amount sometimes referred to as an "equity allowance." The idea is to provide the minister with the equivalent of equity in a home. This is an excellent idea that should be considered by any church having one or more ministers living in church-provided housing. Of course, for the concept to work properly, the equity allowance should not be accessible by the minister until retirement. Therefore, some churches choose to place the allowance directly in a minister's tax-sheltered retirement account.

⊃ **Recommendation.** Equity allowances should also be considered by a church whose minister rents a home.

4. Accountable business expense reimbursement policy. One of the most important components of church staff compensation packages is an "accountable" business expense reimbursement arrangement. This benefit is available to both ministers and lay staff members alike. Under such an arrangement a church (1) reimburses only those business expenses that are properly substantiated within a reasonable time as to date, amount, place, and business purpose, and (2) requires any excess reimbursements (in excess of substantiated expenses) to be returned to the church. Churches should seriously consider adopting an accountable reimbursement policy for reimbursing staff business expenses. Such a policy has the following advantages:

☐ Church staff report their business expenses to the church rather than to the IRS.

☐ Church staff who report their income taxes as employees, or who report as self-employed and who are reclassified as employees by the IRS in an audit, avoid the limitations on the deductibility of employee business expenses. These limitations include (1) the elimination of any deduction if the worker cannot itemize deductions on Schedule A (most taxpayers cannot), and (2) the deductibility of business expenses on Schedule A as an itemized expense only to the extent that these expenses exceed 2% of the worker's adjusted gross income.

☐ The so-called *Deason* allocation rule is avoided. Under this rule, ministers must reduce their business expense deduction by the percentage of their total compensation that consists of a tax-exempt housing allowance.

☐ The "50% limitation" that applies to the deductibility of business meals and entertainment expenses is avoided. Unless these expenses are reimbursed by an employer under an accountable plan, only 50% of them are deductible by either employees or self-employed workers.

☐ Church staff who report their income taxes as self-employed avoid the risk of being reclassified as an employee by the IRS in an audit and assessed additional taxes.

↻ **Observation.** The compensation survey summarized over the next several chapters reveals that many churches provide automobile allowances to their ministers and lay staff. In many cases, a church will simply provide a fixed dollar amount every month to a worker (for example, $300), and require no substantiation of business miles or a return of any "excess reimbursements" (in excess of substantiated business miles). This is referred to as a "nonaccountable" reimbursement arrangement. What are the tax consequences of such an arrangement? The allowances must be added to the worker's W-2 or 1099 at the end of the year, and the worker can claim a business deduction on Schedule A (if an employee) or on Schedule C (if self-employed). If a worker is an employee with insufficient itemized deductions to use Schedule A, there is no deduction available for business expenses even though the full amount of the monthly allowances are added to taxable income. This is a very unfortunate tax result that can be avoided completely through an accountable reimbursement arrangement. For a sample board resolution adopting an accountable business expense reimbursement arrangement, see chapter 7 of Richard Hammar's annual *Church and Clergy Tax Guide.*

The income tax regulations prohibit the funding of accountable reimbursement arrangements through salary reductions.

☞ **Example.** Assume that First Church pays Pastor Gary $500 each week, and also agrees to reimburse his substantiated business expenses for each month out of the first weekly payroll check for the following month. Assume further that Pastor Gary substantiated $300 of business expenses for January. The church issued Pastor Gary his customary check of $500 for the first week of February, but only $200 of this check represents taxable salary while the remaining $300 represents a nontaxable reimbursement under an accountable plan. Only the $200 salary component of this check is included on Pastor Gary's W-2 (or 1099) form at the end of the year. This arrangement was once common, and still is practiced by some churches. The income tax regulations do not prohibit the funding of business expense reimbursements out of salary reductions. Rather, a church's reimbursements under such arrangements cannot be "accountable." This means that a church cannot reduce W-2 income by reducing an employee's salary to pay for business expense reimbursements. In our example, the full $500 paycheck must be accumulated to Pastor Gary's W-2.

↻ **Key point.** Many churches set aside a certain amount each year to cover an employee's total compensation. For ministers, this amount often includes salary, housing allowance, fringe benefits, and an amount for the reimbursement of business expenses. To illustrate, a church board determines in December of 2005 that Pastor Ted's compensation package for 2006 will consist of salary ($30,000), housing allowance ($10,000), fringe benefits ($5,000), and business expense reimbursements ($3,000). This is what is sometimes called a salary "restructuring" arrangement. Are such arrangements treated as salary reductions, meaning that the entire $3,000 must be accumulated to Pastor Ted's W-2 income? Not necessarily. A possible basis exists for not reporting the $3,000 as taxable income to Pastor Ted if all of the following conditions are met: (1) the $3,000 is used to reimburse Pastor Ted for business expenses only if the substantiation requirements of an accountable arrangement are met; (2) the salary "restructuring" occurs prior to the start of the year; (3) any undistributed portion of the $3,000 is not given to Pastor Ted at the end of the year; and (4) the church adopts two resolutions—a "compensation" resolution consisting of salary, housing, and fringe benefits, and a "business expense" resolution consisting of the $3,000 reimbursement amount. If the IRS audits Pastor Ted and asks to see the church resolution specifying his compensation, the church would produce the first resolution. This is an aggressive position that may be rejected by the IRS in an audit. No court has addressed the issue.

5. Travel expenses of a spouse. A church should decide if it will be paying for any of the travel expenses of a spouse accompanying a minister or other staff member on a business trip. Reimbursing these expenses represents a significant benefit. Unfortunately, there is much confusion regarding the correct reporting of such reimbursements for tax purposes. If the spouse's presence on the trip serves a legitimate business purpose, and the spouse's travel expenses are reimbursed by the church under an accountable arrangement (described above) then the reimbursements represent a nontaxable fringe benefit. If these two requirements are not met, the reimbursements represent taxable income to the minister or staff member.

▲ **Caution.** If either of these conditions is not met, then a church's reimbursement of a nonemployee spouse's travel expenses will represent taxable income to the minister or other staff member. The same applies to children who accompany a minister or staff member on a business trip.

✎ **Tax savings tip.** If a church does not reimburse the travel expenses of a pastor's spouse who accompanies the pastor on a business trip, then the spouse may be able to deduct travel expenses as a charitable contribution (assuming that the spouse's presence on the trip serves a legitimate "business" purpose).

6. Church-owned vehicles. Churches should consider the advantages of acquiring an automobile for staff members' church-related travel. Here's why. If a church purchases a car, and the church board adopts a resolution restricting use of the car to church-related activities, then the worker reports no income or deductions, and better yet, there are no accountings, reimbursements, allowances, or recordkeeping requirements. This assumes that the car is in fact used exclusively for church-related purposes, and the strict conditions specified in the income tax regulations are satisfied.

Commuting is always considered to be personal use of a car, and so this procedure would not be available if a church allowed a worker to commute to work in a church-owned vehicle. Fortunately, the income tax regulations permit certain church employees who use a church-owned vehicle exclusively for business purposes except for commuting to receive all of the benefits associated with business use of a church-owned vehicle, if certain additional conditions are met.

Unfortunately, most churches that provide a staff member with a car do not consider either of these alternatives. Rather, they simply transfer the car to the individual and impose no limitations on personal use. This arrangement results in taxable income to the staff member, whether the staff member is a minister or a lay employee. See chapter 4 of Richard Hammar's annual *Church and Clergy Tax Guide* for a full discussion of these rules.

7. Self-employment tax. Social Security benefits are financed through two tax systems. Employers and employees each pay "Social Security" and "Medicare" taxes which for 2006 amount to 7.65% of an employee's taxable wages (a total tax of 15.3%) up to a specified amount. Self-employed persons pay the "self-employment tax," which for 2006 is 15.3% of net self-employment earnings up to a specified amount.

Note that self-employed workers are responsible for paying their entire Social Security tax liability, while employees pay only half (their employer pays the other half).

> ⊃ **Key point.** Ministers always are treated as self-employed for Social Security with respect to services performed in the exercise of their ministry, and so they do not pay "Social Security" and "Medicare" taxes. Rather, they pay the "self-employment tax" with respect to church compensation, unless they have filed a timely application for exemption from Social Security taxes (and received back a copy of their exemption application from the IRS marked "approved"). As a result, ministers must be familiar with the self-employment tax rules. So must lay church employees who work for a church that filed a timely exemption from Social Security coverage (Form 8274), since they are considered self-employed for Social Security.

Because ministers pay a much higher Social Security tax than is required of employees, many churches agree to pay a portion (i.e., one-half) of a minister's self-employment tax liability. This is perfectly appropriate. However, note that any portion of a minister's self-employment tax paid by a church must be reported as additional compensation on the minister's W-2 or 1099 form, and Form 1040. The amount paid by the church must be reported as compensation for Social Security purposes as well.

> ⊃ **Key point.** Housing allowances and the fair rental value of parsonages are includable in self-employment earnings for Social Security purposes.

8. Insurance. Churches often provide ministers with life, health, or disability insurance coverage and pay all of the premiums for such coverage. In some cases, churches make the same benefits available to lay staff members. The income tax regulations specify that the gross income of an *employee* does not include

> contributions which his employer makes to an accident or health plan for compensation (through insurance or otherwise) to the employee for personal injuries or sickness incurred by him, his spouse, or his dependents . . . . The employer may contribute to an accident or health plan by paying the premium (or a portion of the premium) on a policy of accident or health insurance covering one or more of his employees, or by contributing to a separate trust or fund . . . .

The exclusion of employer-paid health insurance premiums from the taxable income of employees is one of the main reasons why ministers and other staff members often are better off reporting their income taxes as employees. This important benefit is not available to workers who report their income taxes as self-employed. A church wishing to make this benefit available to its ministers (or other employees) should adopt a plan in an appropriate board resolution. Plans that benefit only ministers are exempted from the "nondiscrimination" rules that apply to most of these kinds of plans.

> ⊃ **Observation.** The compensation survey data summarized over the next several chapters reveal that many churches provide ministers with health insurance. A smaller percentage of churches provide these benefits to lay staff members. Such "discrimination" by church employers does not violate federal law.

The cost of group term life insurance bought by an employer for its employees ordinarily is not taxable to the employees so long as the amount of coverage does not exceed $50,000 per employee. Generally, life insurance can qualify as group term life insurance only if it is available to at least ten full-time employees. However, there are some exceptions to this rule. For example, the ten full-time employee rule does not apply if (1) an employer provides the insurance to all full-time employees who provide satisfactory evidence of insurability, (2) insurance coverage is based on a uniform percentage of pay, and (3) evidence of insurability is limited to a medical questionnaire completed by the employee that does not require a physical examination.

Other kinds of insurance premiums paid by the church on behalf of a minister or lay church employee ordinarily represent taxable income. For example, the cost of premiums on a whole life or universal life insurance policy paid by a church on the life of its minister (and naming the minister's spouse and children as beneficiaries) ordinarily must be reported as income to the minister.

9. Retirement accounts. Most ministers (and some lay staff members) participate in some form of retirement plan. Such plans often are sponsored either by the local church, or by a denomination or agency with which the church is affiliated. Church workers covered by certain kinds of plans can choose to have part of their pay set aside each year (through "salary reductions") in the retirement fund, rather than receiving it as income. Amounts set aside by the employing church under these plans may be excludable from gross income for tax purposes. These amounts are sometimes called "elective deferrals" because the employee elects to set aside the money, and tax on the money is deferred until it is taken out of the account. This option is available to ministers or lay workers who are covered by tax-sheltered annuities ("403(b) plans"), simplified employee pensions (SEPs), and certain other plans. Payments made by an employing church toward an employee's tax-sheltered annuity, SEP, and certain other plans, and funded out of church funds rather than through a reduction in an employee's compensation, may also be excluded from the employee's gross income for tax purposes under certain circumstances. There are limits on how much an employee can elect to contribute into such plans, and on how much the employing church can contribute out of its own funds. Of course, ministers and lay workers (whether employees or self-employed for income tax purposes) can also contribute to an IRA.

⊃ **Recommendation.** If a church has not established or contributed to a retirement plan for its staff members, then it should consider doing so or at least ensuring that staff members are participating in an adequate alternative (particularly in the case of ministers who have exempted themselves from Social Security coverage). Further, if staff members are participating in a retirement plan, then now is a good time to determine how contributions to the plan in 2006 will be funded (i.e., through employee contributions, salary reductions, or church contributions) and in what amounts.

⊃ **Key point.** Churches that have not adequately contributed to their minister's retirement, or that would like to make contributions in excess of applicable limits, should consider the possible advantages of a "rabbi trust." A church's contributions to such a trust will not be included in a minister's current taxable income, and income generated by the trust is tax-deferred. Further, a church ordinarily can contribute more toward a rabbi trust than to most other kinds of retirement program. This is very attractive for churches whose minister is approaching retirement with inadequate retirement savings. For more information see chapter 10 of Richard Hammar's annual *Church and Clergy Tax Guide*.

10. Works made for hire. It is common for church employees to compose music or write books or articles in their church office during office hours. What is often not understood is that such persons do not necessarily own the copyright in the works they create. While the one who creates a work generally is its author and the initial owner of the copyright in the work, section 201(b) of the Copyright Act specifies that "in the case of a work made for hire, the employer or other person for whom the work was prepared is considered the author . . . and, unless the parties have expressly agreed otherwise in a written instrument signed by them, owns all of the rights comprised in the copyright."

The copyright law defines "work made for hire" as "a work prepared by an employee within the scope of his or her employment." There are two requirements that must be met: (1) the person creating the work is an employee, and (2) the employee created the work within the scope of his or her employment. Whether or not one is an employee will depend on the same factors used in determining whether one is an employee or self-employed for federal income tax reporting purposes (see chapter 2 of Richard Hammar's annual *Church & Clergy Tax Guide*). However, the courts have been very liberal in finding employee status in this context, so it is possible that a court would conclude that a work is a work made for hire even though the author reports federal income taxes as a self-employed person.

The second requirement is that the work must have been created within the scope of employment. This requirement generally means that the work was created during regular working hours, on the employer's premises, using the employer's staff and equipment. This is often a difficult standard to apply. As a result, it is desirable for church employees to discuss this issue with the church leadership to avoid any potential misunderstandings. Section 201(a), quoted above, allows an employer and employee to agree in writing that copyright ownership in works created by the employee within the scope of employment belongs to the employee. This should be a matter for consideration by any church having a minister or other staff member who creates literary or musical works during office hours, on church premises, using church staff and church equipment (e.g., computers, printers, paper, library, secretaries, dictation equipment).

If a church transfers the copyright in a work made for hire to an employee, this may be viewed by the IRS as "private inurement" of the church's resources to an individual. If so, this could jeopardize the church's tax-exempt status. Neither the IRS nor any court has addressed the tax consequences of such an arrangement to a church. Here are some options:

(1) The church transfers copyright ownership to the staff member. This may constitute private inurement. When a church employee writes a book during office hours at the church, using church equipment, supplies, and personnel, the copyright in the work belongs to the church. If the church chooses to renounce its legal rights in the book, and transfers the copyright back to the employee, then it is relinquishing a potentially valuable asset that may produce royalty income for several years. Few if any churches would attempt to "value" the copyright and report it as additional taxable compensation to the employee, and as a result it is hard to avoid the conclusion that such arrangements result in inurement of the church's assets to a private individual. The legal effect is to jeopardize the church's tax-exempt status. While this risk must not be overstated, the consequences would be so undesirable that it should be taken seriously.

> ⊃ **Key point.** Staff members who retain ownership of a work made for hire because of a written transfer signed by the church may be subject to intermediate sanctions (discussed above). Since the church is the legal owner of the copyright in a work made for hire, it is legally entitled to any income generated from sales of the work. By letting the writer or composer retain the copyright, and all rights to royalties, the church in effect is paying compensation to that person in this amount. If the work generates substantial income, then this may trigger intermediate sanctions.

(2) The church retains the copyright. The risk of inurement can be minimized or even avoided if the church retains the copyright in works made for hire, and pays a "bonus" or some other form of compensation that is added to the author's W-2 at the end of the year. This arrangement will not jeopardize the church's tax-exempt status.

(3) The church urges employees to do "outside work" at home. Do you have a writer or composer on staff at your church? If so, it is possible that this person is doing some writing or composing on church premises, using church equipment, during office hours. One way to avoid the problems associated with work made for hire status is to encourage staff members to do all their personal writing and composing at home. Tell staff members that (1) if they do any writing or composing at church during office hours, their works may be

works made for hire; (2) the church owns the copyright in such works; and (3) the church can transfer copyright to the writer or composer, but this may constitute "inurement" of the church's assets to a private individual, jeopardizing the church's tax-exempt status. By urging staff members to do all their personal writing and composing at home the church will also avoid the difficult question of whether works that are written partly at home and partly at the office are works made for hire.

(4) Sermons. It is likely that the courts would consider sermons to be works made for hire, no matter where or when they are written, since they constitute the primary reason that most pastors are hired and therefore represent the essence of the employment relationship.

11. Qualified Tuition Reductions ("QTRs"). Many churches operate elementary or secondary schools, and charge reduced tuition to certain school employees. For example, assume that a church operates an elementary school, charges annual tuition of $2,000, but only charges tuition of $500 for the children of school employees and charges no tuition at all for the child of Pastor Eric (the church's senior minister and president of the school). Such "tuition reductions" are perfectly appropriate. Further, section 117(d) of the federal tax code specifies that they will not result in taxable income to the school employees. In other words, a $500 annual tuition reduction awarded to a school employee whose child attends the school need not be reported as income (on the employee's W-2 or Form 1040). This obviously can be a significant benefit to school employees. However, section 117(d) also provides that "highly compensated employees" cannot exclude qualified tuition reductions from their income unless the same benefit is available on substantially similar terms to other employees. The term "highly compensated employee" is defined to include any employee who was paid compensation for the previous year in excess of a specified amount. For 2005, the amount was $90,000. The amount for 2006 was not available at the time of publication of this text.

If in the example cited above Pastor Eric was paid more than $90,000 for the previous year, then the church would have to include $2,000 (the entire amount of the tuition reduction) in Pastor Eric's reportable income since he is a highly compensated employee and the benefit available to him is not available on substantially similar terms to other employees. However, this will not affect other school employees who are not "highly compensated." They will be able to exclude tuition reductions from their income.

⊃ **Key point.** The IRS has ruled that tuition reductions are tax-free only for school employees, and so if a church operates a private school only employees who perform duties on behalf of the school qualify for this benefit. If the school offers tuition reductions to church employees who perform no duties for the school, these reductions are a taxable fringe benefit.

12. Loans to ministers. Churches often make loans to ministers to enable a minister to pay for housing or some other major purchase. In some cases the church charges no interest or a low rate far below the prevailing market rate of interest. These loans can create problems for a number of reasons. Consider the following.

☐ Many state nonprofit corporation laws prohibit loans to officers and directors. No church should consider making any loan (even at a reasonable rate of interest) to a minister who is an officer or director of the church without first confirming that such loans are permissible under state law.

☐ No-interest or low-interest loans to ministers may be viewed as "inurement" of the church's income to a minister. As noted above, this can potentially jeopardize the church's tax-exempt status.

☐ For loans of $10,000 or more (or for loans of lower amounts where an intent to avoid taxes exists), a church must value the benefit to a minister of receiving a no-interest or low-interest loan and add this amount to the minister's reportable income. This is a complex calculation that is beyond the scope of this book. The point is this—even if loans to ministers are allowed under your state's nonprofit corporation law, the church must recognize that no-interest and low-interest loans of $10,000 or more will result in income to a minister that must be valued and reported (on the minister's W-2 or 1099-MISC, and Form 1040). Failure to do so could result in prohibited "inurement" of the church's income to a private individual, jeopardizing the church's tax-exempt status.

➲ **Observation.** Sadly, some ministers and lay workers never fully repay a loan made to them by their church. The forgiveness of debt ordinarily represents taxable income to the debtor. As a result, if a church makes a loan to a minister or other staff member and the debt is later forgiven by the church, taxable income is generated in the amount of the forgiven debt.

13. Voluntary withholding. Compensation paid to ministers for services performed in the exercise of their ministry is not subject to either income tax or Social Security withholding. This is so whether ministers report their income taxes as employees or as self-employed. As a result, ministers are required to report and prepay their federal taxes by using the estimated tax procedure. This procedure requires ministers to estimate their income tax and self-employment tax liability for the year 2006 prior to April 15, 2006, and then to pay one-fourth of the total estimated tax liability on or by April 15, June 15, September 15, and the following January 15. These quarterly payments are accompanied by a "payment voucher" that is contained in IRS Form 1040-ES. Some ministers find the estimated tax procedure inconvenient and undesirable (it is often hard to budget for the quarterly payments).

Ministers who report their income taxes as employees can enter into a voluntary withholding arrangement with their employing church. Under such an arrangement the employing church withholds income taxes as it would for any other employee, and also an additional amount for the minister's self-employment tax liability (otherwise the minister will need to use the estimated quarterly tax procedure to pay self-employment taxes). The additional amount withheld to cover self-employment taxes must be reported (on the minister's W-2 form and the church's 941 forms) as additional income tax withheld, and not as "Social Security taxes." A minister need only complete and submit to his or her church an IRS Form W-4 to begin voluntary withholding. The arrangement can be terminated by either the minister or the church at any time. Ministers who report their income taxes as self-employed could achieve the same benefit by entering into an unofficial withholding arrangement with their church under which the church withholds amounts from each paycheck to cover the minister's quarterly estimated tax payments. By each quarterly deadline, the church gives the minister the "withheld" compensation to assist him or her in making the quarterly payment. No W-4 should be prepared, since this would be evidence that the minister is in fact an employee. Churches should apprise ministers that they may enter into a voluntary withholding arrangement. For many ministers, such an arrangement will be preferable to the estimated tax procedure.

14. Special occasion gifts. It is common for ministers (and in some cases lay workers) to receive special occasion gifts during the course of the year. Examples include Christmas, birthday, and anniversary gifts. Churches and church staff members often do not understand how to report these payments for federal tax purposes. The general rule is this—if the "gifts" are funded through members' contributions to the church (i.e., the contributions are entered or recorded in the church's books as cash received and the members are given charitable contribution credit) then the distribution to the minister or lay worker should be reported as taxable compensation and included on his or her W-2 or 1099 and Form 1040. The same rule applies to special occasion "gifts" made to a minister or lay worker by the church out of the general fund. Members who contribute to special occasion offerings may deduct their contributions if (1) the contributions are to the church and are entered or recorded in the church's books as cash received, and (2) they are able to itemize deductions on Schedule A (Form 1040). Churches should be prepared to include such "gifts" to a minister or lay worker on his or her W-2 or 1099-MISC. Of course, members are free to make personal gifts to ministers and lay staff members, such as a card at Christmas accompanied by a check or cash. Such payments may be tax-free gifts to the recipient (though they are not deductible by the donor). These same rules apply to other kinds of special occasion gifts as well.

It is common for churches to make generous retirement gifts to retiring ministers (and in some cases lay workers). Do these gifts represent taxable income to the recipient? To the extent that the recipient is an employee (or would be classified as an employee by the IRS), there is no doubt that the "gift" would constitute taxable income. In 1986, section 102(c) was added to the Internal Revenue Code, which specifies that "any amount transferred by or for an employer to or for the benefit of an employee" shall not be excludable from gross income by the employee as a gift, other than certain employee achievement awards and insignificant holiday gifts. Those few ministers and lay workers who in fact are self-employed for income tax reporting purposes have some hope of having a retirement gift characterized as a tax-free gift rather than as taxable compensation for services rendered. Note however that such a conclusion is unlikely given the narrow definition of the term *gift*. The Supreme Court has noted that "a gift in the statutory sense . . . proceeds from a detached and disinterested generosity . . . out of affection, respect, admiration, charity, or like impulses . . . . The most critical consideration . . . is the transferor's intention." *Commissioner v. Duberstein, 363 U.S. 278, 285 (1960)*. The Court also observed that "it doubtless is the exceptional payment by an employer to an employee that amounts to a gift," and that the church's characterization of the distribution as a "gift" is "not determinative—there must be an objective inquiry as to whether what is called a gift amounts to it in reality."

> ⊃ **Key point.** Intermediate sanctions, discussed earlier in this chapter, may apply to a retirement gift that results in unreasonable compensation to the recipient. Church leaders must be sure to consider this possibility before finalizing such a gift. If a retirement gift is excessive, the board members who authorized the gift may be assessed an excise tax equal to 10 percent of the amount by which the gift exceeds reasonable compensation (up to a maximum tax of $10,000, collectively). This is in addition to the excise taxes that may be assessed against the recipient.

15. Bargain sales. Occasionally, a church will sell property to a staff member at a price that is below market value. To illustrate, some churches "sell" a parsonage to a retiring minister at a price well below the property's fair market value. Other churches may sell a car or other church-owned vehicle to a minister at a below-market price. The important consideration with such "bargain sales" is this—the "bargain" element (i.e., the difference between the sales price charged by the church and the property's market value) must be reported as income to the minister on his or her W-2 or 1099-MISC and Form 1040. Churches should consider thoroughly the tax consequences of such sales before approving them.

16. Director immunity. Most states have adopted laws that provide *uncompensated* officers and directors of most charitable organizations (including churches) with limited immunity from legal liability. Congress enacted the Volunteer Protection Act in 1996 that provides similar protection as a matter of federal law. The immunity provided under state and federal law only applies to uncompensated officers and directors. What does this have to do with compensation planning? Simply this—churches should consider adopting an appropriate resolution clarifying that a minister's annual compensation package is for ministerial duties rendered to the church, *and is not for any duties on the church board.* Like any other church officer or director, the minister serves without compensation. Such a provision, if adopted, might qualify the minister for protection under the legal immunity law. It is worth considering.

17. Discretionary funds. It is a fairly common practice for a church to set aside a sum of money in a "discretionary fund" and give the senior minister the sole authority to distribute the money in the fund. In some cases, the minister has no instructions regarding permissible distributions. In other cases, the church establishes guidelines, but these often are oral and ambiguous. Many churches are unaware of the tax consequences of such arrangements. To the extent the minister has the authority to use any portion of the discretionary fund for his or her own personal use, then the entire fund must be reported as taxable income to the minister in the year it is funded. This is so even if the minister does not personally benefit from the fund. The mere fact that the minister *could* personally benefit from the fund is enough for the fund to constitute taxable income. The basis for this result is the "constructive receipt" rule, which is explained in the income tax regulations as follows:

> Income although not actually reduced to a taxpayer's possession is constructively received by him in the taxable year during which it is credited to his account, set apart for him, or otherwise made available so that he may draw upon it at any time, or so that he could have drawn upon it during the taxable year if notice of intention to withdraw had been given. However, income is not constructively received if the taxpayer's control of its receipt is subject to substantial limitations or restrictions.

For a discretionary fund to constitute taxable income to a minister, it is essential that the minister have the authority to "draw upon it at any time" for his or her own personal use. This means that the fund was established without any express prohibition against personal distributions. On the other hand, if a discretionary fund is set up by a board resolution that absolutely prohibits any distribution of the fund for the minister's personal use, then the constructive receipt rule is avoided. In the words of the regulation, "income is not constructively received if the taxpayer's control of its receipt is subject to substantial limitations or restrictions." Accordingly, in order to avoid the reporting of the entire discretionary fund as taxable income to the minister, it is essential that the fund be established by means of a board or congregational resolution that absolutely prohibits any use of the fund by the minister for personal purposes. Further, the resolution should specify that the fund may be distributed by the minister only for needs or projects that are consistent with the church's exempt purposes (as set forth in the church's charter). For accountability purposes, a member of the church board should review all distributions from the discretionary fund to be sure that these requirements are met.

18. Severance pay. Many churches have entered into severance pay arrangements with a pastor or other staff member. Such arrangements can occur when a pastor or staff member is dismissed, retires, or voluntarily resigns. Church treasurers must determine whether severance pay is taxable so that it can be properly reported (on a W-2 and the church's 941 forms). Also, taxes must be withheld from severance pay that is paid to nonminister employees (and ministers who have elected voluntary withholding). Failure to properly report severance pay can result in substantial penalties for both a church and the recipient.

In most cases severance pay represents taxable income to the recipient. There is one exception that will apply in some cases. The tax code excludes from taxable income "the amount of any damages received (whether by suit or agreement and whether as lump sums or as periodic payments) *on account of personal injuries or sickness*." According to this provision, severance pay that is intended to settle personal injury claims may be nontaxable. The words "personal injuries" are defined broadly by the IRS and the courts, and include potential or threatened lawsuits based on discrimination and harassment.

> ⊃ **Key point.** The Tax Court has noted that "payments for terminating and canceling employment contracts are not payments for personal injuries."

Here are some factors to consider (based on actual cases) in deciding whether a severance payment made to a former worker represents taxable compensation or nontaxable damages in settlement of a personal injury claim: (1) An amount paid to a former employee "to reward her for her past services and to make her severance as amicable as possible" is taxable compensation. (2) An amount paid to a former employee under a severance agreement that contains no reference to a specific discrimination or other personal injury claim is taxable compensation. (3) If an employer pays a former employee severance pay, and reports the severance pay on a W-2 (or 1099), this is strong evidence that the amount represents taxable compensation. (4) If an employer continues one or more employee benefits (such as health insurance) as part of a severance agreement, this suggests that any amount payable under the agreement represents taxable compensation. (5) If an employer withholds taxes from amounts paid under a severance agreement, this "is a significant factor" in classifying the payments as taxable income. Of course, this factor will not be relevant in the case of ministers whose wages are not subject to withholding (unless they elect voluntary withholding). (6) Referring to a payment as "severance pay" indicates that it is taxable compensation rather than nontaxable damages in settlement of a personal injury claim. (7) Severance pay based on a former employee's salary (such as one year's salary) is more likely to be viewed as taxable compensation rather than nontaxable damages in settlement of a personal injury claim. (8) To be nontaxable, severance pay must represent "damages" received in settlement of a personal injury claim. The IRS has noted that this language requires more than a settlement agreement in which a former employee "waives" any discrimination or other personal injury claims he or she may have against an employer. If the employee "never filed a lawsuit or any other type of claim against [the employer] . . . the payment cannot be characterized as damages for personal injuries" since "there is no indication that personal injuries actually exist."

19. Income "splitting." Some ministers have attempted to "split" their church income with their spouse. This often is done to qualify the spouse for Social Security or other benefits or to avoid the Social Security "annual earnings test" (which reduces Social Security benefits to retired workers who are under "full retirement age" who earn more than an amount prescribed by law). For income splitting arrangements to work, the courts have required proof that the spouse is in fact an employee of the church. This means that the spouse performs meaningful services on behalf of the church. The courts have pointed to a number of factors indicating that a spouse is *not* an employee: (1) The spouse did not receive a paycheck. (2) The spouse was not employed elsewhere. (3) The spouse's "compensation" was designed to provide a tax benefit (such as an IRA contribution), and lacked any economic reality. (4) Neither the church nor the minister documented any of the services the spouse performed. (5) Neither the church nor the minister could explain how the spouse's "salary" was determined. (6) There was no employment contract between the church and the minister's spouse. (7) No taxes were withheld from the spouse's "salary." (8) The spouse's income was not reported on the church's employment tax returns (Forms 941). (9) There was no evidence that wages were actually paid to the spouse, or that any employment contract existed, or that the spouse was treated as an employee.

The courts generally have been skeptical of attempts by taxpayers to shift income to a spouse. The message is clear—ministers should not attempt to obtain tax benefits by shifting income to a spouse unless there is economic reality to the arrangement.

Compensation Checklist For 2006

Item	Recommendations
salary	• avoid unreasonable compensation • avoid use of salary reductions that are not recognized by federal tax law
housing allowance	• for ministers who own or rent their home, designate a portion of their compensation as a housing allowance prior to December 31 for the next year • for ministers who live in a church-owned parsonage, designate a portion of their compensation as a parsonage allowance (if they will incur any housing expenses) prior to December 31 for the next year
equity allowance	• consider contributing to a tax-sheltered investment (such as a retirement fund) for ministers who live in church-owned parsonage, to compensate for their inability to accumulate equity in a home
accountable business expense reimbursement arrangement	• adopt an accountable business expense reimbursement arrangement by reimbursing only those business expenses that are adequately substantiated, and by requiring any excess reimbursements to be returned
travel expenses of a spouse	• reimburse a spouse's travel expenses incurred in accompanying a minister or lay employee on a business trip if the spouse's presence serves a legitimate business purpose and the expenses are duly substantiated (if these requirements are not met, then the church's reimbursements represent taxable income to the minister or lay employee)
church-owned vehicles	• avoid allowing minister or lay employee unrestricted personal use of a church-owned car (such usage must be valued and reported as taxable income) • consider adopting a policy limiting use of the car to business purposes and requiring it to be kept on church property (this avoids most recordkeeping requirements and does not result in any income to the minister) • an alternative is to limit use of the car to business purposes except for commuting to and from work (if the commuting is required for security reasons); each round trip commute represents $3 of reportable income
self-employment tax paid by church	• all ministers are self-employed for Social Security purposes with respect to their church work; this means they pay the self-employment tax rather than FICA taxes • some churches pay a portion of a minister's self-employment tax (as they pay a portion of a nonminister employee's FICA taxes); such payments represent taxable income • nonminister employees of churches that waived payment of FICA taxes by filing a timely Form 8274 are treated as self-employed for Social Security purposes—churches may want to pay a portion of the self-employment taxes owed by these workers if they do so for ministers
insurance	• consider paying health insurance premiums for ministers and lay employees (a tax-free fringe benefit for employees) • consider paying premiums for up to $50,000 of group term life insurance (a tax-free fringe benefit for employees)
retirement accounts	• consider contributing toward a tax-sheltered retirement plan

works made for hire	• urge staff members to write books and articles
qualified tuition reductions	• consider tuition discounts for ministers and lay employees whose children attend church-operated schools or preschools (they may be a tax-free fringe benefit)
loans to ministers	• avoid making any low or no interest loan to ministers • avoid making any loan to ministers at market rates unless permitted by state nonprofit corporation law
voluntary withholding	• ministers and lay workers who report their income taxes as employees should consider entering into a voluntary withholding arrangement wit the church (can avoid the quarterly estimated tax procedure); be sure to provide for the withholding of self-employment taxes too, but classify these extra withholdings as additional income taxes
special occasion gifts	• special occasion gifts to ministers and lay employees that are processed through the church's books, and for which contribution credit is given to donors, are taxable income to the minister or lay employee
bargain sales	• any property sold to a minister or lay employee at less than fair market value will result in taxable income (the amount by which the fair market value exceeds the sales price)
director immunity	• consider adopting a board resolution certifying that all church board members, including the senior minister, serve without compensation (this may qualify the minister for the limited immunity the law provides to uncompensated directors of nonprofit organizations)
discretionary funds	• avoid them unless (1) the minister cannot use the fund for his or her own personal use, (2) the fund may be distributed only for purposes consistent with the church's exempt purposes, and (3) a board member reviews all distributions to ensure compliance with these limits
severance pay	• severance pay is perfectly appropriate, but be sure that it is reported as additional taxable income unless it represents payment *on account of personal injuries or sickness*
income "splitting"	• do not attempt to shift a portion of a minister's compensation to his or her spouse for tax savings purposes, unless there is "economic reality" to the arrangement (the spouse performs services that otherwise would be compensated, and receives a reasonable rate of compensation)

Chapter 3

Using the Compensation Tables

The following chapters present compensation patterns for nine major positions within the local church. These profiles are the statistical heart of the *Compensation Handbook*. This chapter is designed to help you interpret the tables and maximize your use of the information in this book.

Each staff position has its own chapter including both compensation tables and a discussion of the findings. The tables are for full-time staff members, except for the last table in each chapter which provides data for part-time staff members. A comparative summary of all the positions is presented in Chapter 4.

Interpreting the Tables

Each chapter contains tables that portray compensation averages according to several key variables. The variables include the following:

- ❏ Church attendance (Sunday morning worship)
- ❏ Church income (from all sources)
- ❏ Attendance and setting[1]
- ❏ Gender
- ❏ Education
- ❏ Years employed (in current position)

Each table provides several columns of averages for the following compensation items:

- ❏ Salary—annual base salary
- ❏ Annual % Increase—the percent increase of base salary for the last year
- ❏ Parsonage—rental value of parsonage plus other housing expenses
- ❏ Housing—amount of housing allowance provided for the purchase or rent of a home and its up-keep and furnishings

---

[1]   Five settings are used: urban, suburban, medium size city, small town, rural. Each respondent was permitted to use his or her own judgment in defining their setting. The same approach is followed in using the tables. Each user must determine his or her own setting.

❑ Retirement—money church provides for retirement, not including social security payments

❑ Life Insurance—cost of life insurance provided for staff member as a benefit

❑ Health Insurance—cost of health insurance provided for staff member as a benefit

❑ Vacation/weeks—number of weeks of paid vacation

❑ Auto Allowance— the percentage of staff members receiving an auto allowance

❑ Education Funds—amount provided for continuing education

Immediately following the listing for the compensation item is a percentage. That percentage indicates the proportion of staff members who receive that benefit. For example, consider the following example taken from Chapter 5:

Table 5-3: Annual Compensation Of Senior Pastors By Church Setting And Size

Attendance 0-250	Urban	Suburban	Medium City	Small Town	Rural
Number Of Respondents	48	119	73	156	60
Salary (100%*)	33,883	34,875	34,845	31,371	30,686
Annual % Increase (63%)	4%	5%	5%	4%	4%
Parsonage (16%)	8,702	17,890	14,427	9,703	8,240

Notice that (100%) follows *Salary*. This indicates that 100% of the respondents received a salary. In some tables, less than 100% of the respondents may receive a salary, indicating that they receive their compensation in other ways, For example, a pastor of a small church may receive his or her total compensation as a housing allowance and fringe benefits. Following *Parsonage* is (16%). This means that 16% of all senior pastors lived in a church provided parsonage. In the first column on the *Parsonage* line is the figure 8,702. This means that of the 16% of all senior pastors who received a parsonage allowance, those that serve urban churches with an attendance between 0-250 received on average an allowance of $8,702.

Total Compensation Comparisons

Below each table is a smaller box that lists the *average compensation* for each category. The *average compensation* includes the sum of the base salary, the housing or parsonage allowance, retirement contributions, life and health insurance payments, and educational funds. *This is the key figure for compensation analysis.* The following information is also found in the *Total Compensation Comparisons* box.

Standard Deviation

Following the average compensation is the standard deviation. The standard deviation is the most important and widely used measure of dispersion. In a normal distribution, one standard deviation away from the average represents 68.27% of all responses. For example, in this study the average compensation for pastors was $74,969. The standard deviation was $29,256. Thus, approximately 68% of all pastors receive a compensation falling between $45,713 (74,969 - 29,256) and $104,225 (74,969 + 29,256). A range of two standard deviations on either side of the average encompasses 95% of responses.

25

Median Income

Included in the *Total Compensation Comparisons* box is the median income for each reporting category. The median income represents the compensation amount below which 50% of the compensation totals fall. In essence, it divides the participants into two groups having equal frequency. For the purpose of this book, however, when the reporting category has an even number of participants, the median income that is reported is the compensation of the person representing N/2 (the total number of participants divided by two).

National Average

Included in the *Total Compensation Comparisons* box is the national average. This figure represents the average compensation nationwide for that position.

Rounding Errors

Rounding errors may exist in some of the data in this study. They do not, however, impact the final results in any significant way. Some of the hourly wages for part-time workers may deviate a few cents due to rounding errors.

Using the Tables To Plan Compensation

The most important use of this handbook is for compensation planning. The following example illustrates one approach of how this book can be used.

Example: Planning the Compensation of a Senior Pastor

> *Reverend West has served as senior pastor of Maywood Church for the past nine years. Maywood Church is a suburban congregation with an average Sunday worship attendance of 395, and an annual budget of $775,000. Reverend West has a Master of Divinity degree.*

The above example provides us with relevant data that can be used in coordination with the tables in this book. Church income is the single most important variable, followed by attendance, in predicting compensation. Other factors that we will use include the geographical setting of the church (in this case suburban), plus the pastor's length of service (nine years) and educational background (Master of Divinity degree).

> ⊃ **Key point.** The goal is not to come up with a single compensation number, but rather to identify a *base compensation range*. Once that range is determined, a variety of factors will affect the final choice of a specific level of compensation.

Step 1. The first step is to use the Tables in Chapter 5 to identify the *average base compensation range* for senior pastors in settings comparable to those of Reverend West. We begin by examining *church attendance* (Table 5-1), *church income* (Table 5-2), and *church attendance and geographical setting* (which for this example is Table 5-4: suburban churches with an attendance between 251-500). The main data we are interested in is found at the bottom of each table in the box labeled *Total Compensation Comparisons*. There we find data that summarizes the average church attendance, income, years employed, and compensation for the participants detailed in each column of each table. We also find the standard deviation for each column (for more information on standard deviations, see page 33). The relevant data from Tables 5-1, 5-2, and 5-4 are summarized below. In addition, the table below presents the average per capita giving.

1. Data for example	2. Average church attendance	3. Average church income	4. Average per capita giving	5. Average compensation	6. Standard deviation	7. Range based on one standard deviation (encompasses 68% of all respondents)
Maywood Church	395	$775,000	$1,962	to be determined		
Table 5-1 300-499	375	$732,267	$1,953	$82,586	$21,883	$60,703 - $104,469
Table 5-2 750,000 - 999,999	420	$855,158	$2,036	$85,669	$22,427	$63,242 - $108,096
Table 5-4 (Suburban)	368	$738,537	$2,007	$86,475	$22,375	$64,100 - 108,850

The above table enables us to establish two important compensation ranges. The first is based on the average compensation (column 5). The data from Tables 5-1, 5-2, and 5-5 provide us with a range of *average compensation* between $82,586 on the low end to $86,475 on the high end. These figures serve as an *average base compensation range*. The second important range is based on the standard deviation totals found in column 7. The *standard deviation range* indicates that 68% of pastors in similar settings have a compensation that falls between $60,703 on the low end to $108,850 on the high end. Going to the second standard deviation range could push the upper compensation amount to over $131,000 based on the data found in Table 5-4. Based on this data, we will begin by using the *average base compensation range* of $82,586 - $86,475. Other factors will then determine if that range should be modified.

Since church income is the most important factor in determining compensation, let's begin by focusing on column 3. First, we see that the average church income for Maywood Church is slightly higher than the amounts for Table 5-1 and Table 5-4, but lower than the amount for Table 5-2. As a result, church income does not appear to be a significant factor in making an adjustment to the base compensation range.

In column 4 we note that the per capita giving for Maywood Church is very close to that of Table 5-1, but slightly below that of Table 5-2 and Table 5-4. It does not appear that per capita giving has a significant impact on adjusting the compensation range.

Finally, we note that Maywood Church's attendance, found in column 1, is quite similar to the average attendance found in the other three tables. Overall, we can conclude that Maywood church is quite similar in most respects to the data found in the three tables.

These conclusions suggest that the base compensation range of $82,586 - $86,475 fits the profile of Maywood Church fairly well. Next, let's look at two variations of our example and consider the resulting implications for the base compensation range.

Variation 1. First, let's change Maywood Church's income from $775,000 to $950,000. This produces a per capita giving of $2,405. The income and giving would then be higher than the averages from Tables 5-1, 5-2 and 5-4. That suggests that Reverend West's *base compensation range* might be increased beyond the upper limit of $86,475. How much beyond will depend on the factors that we examine in Steps 2-4.

Variation 2. Next, suppose that Maywood Church's income drops to $650,000. That results in a per capita income of $1,646. Both the income and the per capita giving would be below the national averages presented above. That suggests that Reverend West's compensation may be lower than than the average range taken from column five. The final determination would depend on several of the factors that we examine below.

After establishing a base compensation range, the next step is to determine if Reverend West's final compensation should fit within that range, and if so where, or if the comepnsation should go beyond or below that range based upon other key factors such as education, length of service, and congregational values.

In making the final determination, the standard deviation range provides us with some working boundaries on both the upper and lower limits. Since, on initial observation, there is nothing extraordinary about Maywoord Church's profile, in all likelihood, Reverend West's compensation will fall within the first standard deviation range found in Tables 5-1 and 5-2.

Step 2. The second step is to examine additional factors that might impact compensation such as *education* and *years of service*. This requires an examination of Table 5-9 (*Annual Compensation Of Senior Pastors by Education*) and Table 5-10 (*Annual Compensation of Senior Pastors by Years Employed*). These factors do not have as strong a correlation with compensation as do church income and attendance. As such, they are less useful in establishing a compensation range, but are helpful in deciding whether an individual is in the upper or lower parts of the range identified in Step 1.

1. Profile of Rev. West: M.Div. 9 years	2. Average church attendance	3. Average years of service	4. Average church income	5. Average per capita giving	6. Average compensation	7. Standard deviation	8. Range based on one standard deviation
Maywood Church	395	9	$775,000	$1,962	to be determined		
Table 5-9 Master's Degree	453	10	$841,186	$1,857	$77,341	$29,904	$47,437 - $107,245
Table 5-10 6-10 years of service	402	8	$775,015	$1,928	$74,184	$31,141	$43,043 - $105,325

In column 6 above, we find that the average compensation for pastors with a master's degree is very close to the national average ($77,341 compared to $77,096). In addition, their average church income and attendance is above that of Maywood Church. Similarly, those with 6-10 years of service, such as Pastor West, receive an annual compensation almost identical to the national average ($74,184 compared to $77,096). So, based on the data for Reverend West, no significant differential exists based on either education or years of service.

Variation 1. Suppose Pastor West has a doctoral degree. On average, senior pastors with a doctorate earn approximately $12,000 above the national average (see Table 5-9 in Chapter 5). In part this is because they serve larger churches with higher incomes. The average compensation for those with a doctorate is $89,217. This falls just above the range we identified from Step 1 ($82,586 - $86,475). The average church attendance for those with doctorates is 548, which is higher than Maywood Church's average of 395, and the average church income of $1,166,938 is well above that of Maywood's $775,000. So all things considered, the compensation range from Step 1 would still serve us fairly well even in Rev. West had a doctoral degree. Nevertheless, a doctoral degree is a relevant factor that suggests higher levels of compensation are normal. How much higher will vary from one situation to another. In this case it would be a positive factor that might suggest moving toward or above the higher end of the range from Step 1 rather than the lower end of the range.

Variation 2. What if Reverend West's educational level is lower than a Master of Divinity degree? It would probably have little impact. The reason is that Maywood Church has an average income and attendance that is well above that of most churches with pastors that have less education, and church income and attendance are the strongest factors that correlate with pastoral compensation. As a result, even with less education (or years of service), the compensation range established in Step 1 still applies.

Step 3. The third step is to take into account the unique circumstances that define each individual situation. One factor is the cost of living for your area. Is it higher or lower than the national average? Your local Chamber of Commerce or a real estate agency can help you obtain that information. Other factors such as denominational affiliation (see Table 4-12), theological beliefs, pastoral performance, financial needs, goodwill, the local economy, personal motivation, congregational goals, internal church politics, and many other considerations will also contribute to the final decision. For some churches that may mean a final compensation package much lower or much higher than the projected range listed in Step 1. How that compensation will be divided up will vary greatly from one church to another, and even from one individual staff member to another. Care should be given, however, to avoid gender discrimination. This is a widespread problem involving many churches (see Table 4-8). In addition, a large disparity between the pastor's compensation, and that of other staff members, can have an impact on the rate of increase that the pastor may experience in future years. Often, once a staff member has reached the upper limits of his or her compensation range, future raises may be somewhat smaller in order to better compensate other staff members.

Step 4. The final step is to examine the *standard deviation* range for all senior pastors. Use Table 4-3 found in Chapter 4. That table indicates that the compensation of 95% of all pastors is less than $140,272 and that 68% of pastors earn less than $108,684. Thus, the final determination of Reverend West's compensation may significantly exceed the average range taken from column 5 of $82,586 - $86,475 without being unreasonable. Both tangible and intangible factors will impact the selection of the final compensation package. One concern is to make certain that the final compensation total does not fall so far outside of the normal distribution of clergy compensation that the church could possibly lose its tax exempt status due to payments that the tax court might consider "unreasonable" (see the discussion on *Salary* in Chapter 2). Naturally, those in the largest churches will have standard deviations that boost the upper limit above the $140,000 mark for two standard deviations. Appendix 5 graphically displays the standard deviation ranges of pastoral compensation based on church income.

The final determination of compensation is unique to every congregation. It would not be surprising to see a range of compensation for Reverend West somewhere between $70,000 - $95,000. Higher compensation levels are possible, and could be argued to be reasonable. It would be unlikely, however, for Reverend West to exceed $110,000, which would fall outside the limits of the second standard deviation range for churches similar to Maywood Church. Such a compensation level would require independent justification to avoid the possibility of intermediate sanctions (see Chapter 2 for a discussion of intermediate sanctions).

This same process can be used for each of the nine staff positions found in this handbook.

Chapter 4

Compensation Profiles: General Comparisons

This chapter provides comparisons of the average compensations for the nine staff positions included in this study. A summary table exists for each of the variables examined. More detailed analysis can be found in the individual chapter for each staff position.

As expected, pastors consistently rank first in total compensation for church staff members. Associate pastors received the second highest compensation amount followed generally by music and choir directors. The tables presented later in this chapter provide compensation rankings and comparisons according to the national averages for each position.

What factors determine compensation?

Church income, attendance, geographical setting, and the gender of the staff member were the four most important factors affecting total compensation. While no single factor played the decisive role, female staff members consistently received lower compensation than did their male counterparts.

Church income and attendance proved to be the most important variables affecting compensation for each of the nine positions examined in this study. Yet, the correlation between these variables and employee compensation accounts for only part of the variation in compensation amounts for these positions. These factors, while important, must be viewed in the context of other factors, the combination of which ultimately determine compensation. For example, theology may play a significant role in some churches in the determination of compensation. The compensation of a Catholic priest who has taken a vow of poverty will be low regardless of church size or income. In churches that promote financial prosperity as a sign of God's blessing, the pastor may receive a disproportionate amount of the church's total income. Politics and power may prove the decisive factors in determining compensation in a church embroiled in conflict. A building program may be the controlling factor somewhere else. In general, education, geographical setting, and years of service play some role in almost every church. Unfortunately, significant gender gaps existed for every position. While some of these gaps can be explained on the basis of demographic factors such as church setting or personal education, the conclusion cannot be escaped that gender discrimination is widespread within the church concerning compensation and the access to higher paying positions. The largest compensation gap between men and women was for church administrators—on average, for this position, females earned 65% of the compensation of males.

General Trends

This study examined the "rate of increase" with respect to compensation and church attendance, and compensation and church income. In this context, "rate of increase" refers to how fast compensation rose with respect to church attendance or size of church budget. For most staff positions, the rate of increase for total compensation was the highest for churches with an attendance below 300 and over 750.

Church bookkeepers, secretaries, and custodians experienced only modest compensation growth increase as the church size increased. Like the other positions, compensation grows more slowly in churches with an attendance between 200 to 750. Some compensation growth appeared for larger churches, but even then, their total compensation was considerably less than the other church staff positions.

Similar trends could be seen based upon church income. Pastoral compensation increased at every budget level. Associate pastors, CE directors, and youth ministers experienced only modest increases in compensation for budgets between $250,000 and $750,000. The compensation for choir directors and administrators rose more rapidly. Bookkeepers, secretaries, and custodians did not fare as well. They experienced only modest increases as church income rose, with bookkeepers and custodians doing slightly better than secretaries.

Benefit Comparison

Benefits vary significantly from one position to the next. This was especially true for the more important benefits of health insurance and retirement programs. Only 37 to 79 percent of church staff have health insurance and fewer have retirement benefits. Bookkeepers, custodians, and secretaries are less likely to receive benefits than are the other professional staff members. Part-time staff members receive few fringe benefits. The tables below provide benefit comparisons (please note that some position titles and benefit listings have been abbreviated).

Table 4-1: Percentage of Full-time Staff Receiving Benefits

	Pastor	Associate	CE Dir.	Youth	Music	Admin.	Book.	Secretary	Custodian
raise	67%	73%	73%	71%	72%	73%	77%	59%	76%
parsonage	15%	7%	4%	6%	3%	2%	0%	0%	1%
housing	82%	81%	54%	70%	61%	28%	1%	0%	1%
retirement	67%	62%	52%	54%	55%	47%	44%	24%	35%
life ins.	36%	41%	37%	37%	44%	34%	36%	12%	35%
health ins.	79%	79%	70%	78%	71%	65%	56%	37%	63%
vacation	93%	95%	90%	94%	91%	91%	95%	87%	88%
education	45%	44%	43%	39%	36%	33%	17%	17%	6%
auto allow.	85%	87%	89%	88%	86%	85%	81%	26%	75%

Table 4-2: Percentage of Part-time Staff Receiving Benefits

	Pastor	Associate	CE Dir.	Youth	Music	Admin.	Book.	Secretary	Custodian
raise	37%	50%	60%	44%	55%	55%	60%	41%	45%
parsonage	27%	4%	2%	1%	1%	0%	0%	0%	0%
housing	53%	57%	8%	14%	6%	5%	0%	0%	1%
retirement	13%	7%	9%	5%	6%	16%	7%	7%	2%
life ins.	3%	9%	5%	5%	2%	5%	6%	1%	2%
health ins.	20%	26%	10%	10%	4%	16%	6%	4%	4%
vacation	57%	57%	45%	47%	36%	52%	33%	56%	29%
education	30%	32%	24%	15%	11%	12%	5%	8%	0%
auto allow.	37%	81%	59%	52%	47%	63%	56%	12%	43%

Note: the following tables are for comparative purposes only. For a full analysis of each staff position, consult chapters 5-13.

Table 4-3: National Church Staff Compensation Averages

Position	Average Compensation*	Standard Deviation	X æ 1 (68%)	X æ 2 (95%)
Pastor	77,096	31,588	45,508 - 108,684	13,920 - 140,272
Associate Pastor	64,034	26,369	37,665 - 90,403	11,296 - 116,772
Music Choir Dir.	60,316	20,343	39,973 - 80,659	19,630 - 101,002
Administrator	53,153	22,489	30,664 - 75,642	8,175 - 98,131
CE Director	51,983	18,468	33,515 - 70,451	15,047 - 88,919
Youth Minister	50,371	15,112	35,259 - 65,483	20,147 - 80,595
Bookkeeper	33,336	11,181	22,155 - 44,517	10,974 - 55,698
Custodian	31,026	11,695	19,331 - 42,721	7,636 - 54,416
Secretary	26,624	9,849	16,775 - 36,473	6,926 - 46,322

* The average compensation includes base salary, housing or parsonage allowance, retirement contribution, life and health insurance payments, and educational funds.

Using the Standard Deviation

In a normal distribution, one standard deviation away from the average represents 68.27% of all responses. For example, in this study the average compensation for pastors was $77,096. The standard deviation was $31,588. Thus, approximately 68% of all pastors receive a compensation falling between $45,508 (77,096 - 31,588) and $108,684 (77,096 + 31,588). A range of two standard deviations on either side of the average encompasses 95% of responses. The standard deviations listed in the table above apply only to national averages for each position and not to the other tables in this chapter.

Table 4-4: Annual Church Staff Compensation Averages by Church Attendance*

Attendance	0-99	100-299	300-499	500-749	750-999	over 1,000
Pastor	46,509	66,461	81,407	94,398	102,334	115,577
Associate Pastor	31,986	49,430	58,280	67,806	68,402	82,016
CE Director	31,254	37,036	46,697	51,613	51,364	63,085
Youth Minister		42,308	48,740	49,692	54,218	58,470
Music/Choir Dir.		50,048	50,451	59,481	61,035	72,620
Administrator	20,607	35,268	42,688	55,896	59,243	70,662
Bookkeeper		30,995	28,779	32,560	34,472	37,586
Secretary	22,040	24,495	26,800	27,829	29,994	31,667
Custodian		23,857	27,381	32,056	34,162	36,100

* The average compensation includes base salary, housing or parsonage allowance, retirement contribution, life and health insurance payments, and educational funds.

Table 4-5: Annual Church Staff Compensation Averages by Church Income*

Church Budget in $	0-249,999	250,000-499,999	500,000-749,000	750,000-999,999	1,000,000 +
Pastor	52,362	67,420	77,915	85,669	106,337
Associate Pastor	43,758	48,778	57,832	57,461	73,647
CE Director	37,477	33,812	45,834	45,533	56,860
Youth Minister	45,587	41,265	47,399	48,293	54,361
Music/Choir Dir.	55,627	41,912	51,061	51,846	66,390
Administrator	41,186	34,711	38,657	37,998	63,841
Bookkeeper	27,655	23,531	27,814	28,950	36,185
Secretary	21,108	25,507	27,066	27,303	31,622
Custodian	23,672	22,172	25,824	29,799	33,909

* The average compensation includes base salary, housing or parsonage allowance, retirement contribution, life and health insurance payments, and educational funds.

Table 4-6: Annual Church Staff Compensation Averages by Church Setting and Size*

Attendance Under 500	Urban	Suburban	Medium City	Small Town	Rural
Pastor	69,790	74,446	66,545	57,025	49,474
Associate Pastor	40,504	50,564	47,796	40,544	39,668
CE Director	48,659	46,426	38,020	39,398	
Youth Minister	41,762	48,935	45,365	44,753	40,909
Music/Choir Dir.	54,254	49,225	50,090	47,963	
Administrator	44,416	41,176	37,860	33,430	35,172
Bookkeeper	34,186	32,854	28,708	22,848	
Secretary	28,730	26,774	24,955	23,703	22,114
Custodian	28,672	27,962	25,888	22,119	

* The average compensation includes base salary, housing or parsonage allowance, retirement contribution, life and health insurance payments, and educational funds.

Table 4-7: Annual Church Staff Compensation Averages by Church Setting and Size*

Attendance over 499	Urban	Suburban	Medium City	Small Town	Rural
Pastor	110,039	109,441	100,118	95,442	86,237
Associate Pastor	77,939	72,680	67,525	75,913	51,437
CE Director	59,321	58,795	54,576	55,038	43,584
Youth Minister	54,517	56,954	54,341	45,767	50,918
Music/Choir Dir.	65,840	70,356	64,051	55,324	50,118
Administrator	68,065	65,971	60,468	54,814	53,204
Bookkeeper	37,067	37,136	34,200	31,055	
Secretary	32,951	31,713	27,942	25,490	24,671
Custodian	36,408	34,904	35,136	28,057	34,100

* The average compensation includes base salary, housing or parsonage allowance, retirement contribution, life and health insurance payments, and educational funds.

Table 4-8: Annual Church Staff Compensation Averages by Gender *

Gender	Male	Female	F/M Ratio
Pastor	77,550	62,690	81%
Associate Pastor	65,752	48,763	74%
CE Director	61,239	41,664	68%
Youth Minister	50,984	42,515	83%
Music/Choir Dir.	62,070	48,334	78%
Administrator	64,402	38,833	60%
Bookkeeper	35,817	33,110	92%
Secretary	30,429	26,574	87%
Custodian	32,523	23,311	72%

* The average compensation includes base salary, housing or parsonage allowance, retirement contribution, life and health insurance payments, and educational funds.

Table 4-9: Annual Church Staff Compensation Averages by Education*

Highest Degree	High School	Associate	Bachelor	Master	Doctorate
Pastor	63,625	49,471	67,411	77,341	89,217
Associate Pastor	48,906	44,790	61,325	69,283	68,175
CE Director	36,956	48,039	47,443	61,440	68,689
Youth Minister	44,805	43,321	47,819	57,062	
Music/Choir Dir.	50,442	55,511	57,712	63,643	78,062
Administrator	38,038	40,778	54,126	68,093	58,757
Bookkeeper	31,452	33,134	35,207	37,881	
Secretary	25,577	26,750	28,483	27,919	
Custodian	31,034	35,404	34,031	27,343	

* The average compensation includes base salary, housing or parsonage allowance, retirement contribution, life and health insurance payments, and educational funds.

Table 4-10: Annual Church Staff Compensation Averages by Years Employed*

Years Employed	0-5	6-10	11-15	over 15
Pastor	71,107	74,184	85,240	85,386
Associate Pastor	60,562	65,874	69,478	72,791
CE Director	49,910	54,491	53,816	61,021
Youth Minister	48,108	57,365	54,454	54,510
Music/Choir Dir.	56,682	61,801	62,809	71,261
Administrator	50,467	55,727	61,353	52,594
Bookkeeper	32,971	30,781	34,086	38,817
Secretary	24,903	27,945	28,609	28,343
Custodian	28,980	30,449	33,449	36,385

* The average compensation includes base salary, housing or parsonage allowance, retirement contribution, life and health insurance payments, and educational funds.

Table 4-11: Annual Hourly Compensation Averages for Part-Time Church Staff*

Hours per week	1-14	15-29	30-39	All Part-time
Pastor	27.86	53.84	20.03	27.82
Associate Pastor	12.92	18.84	20.18	18.99
CE Director	12.80	13.73	17.06	14.30
Youth Minister	20.84	14.50	12.07	16.00
Music/Choir Dir.	23.08	16.52	17.53	16.64
Administrator		17.91	19.33	16.14
Bookkeeper	12.56	11.55	17.07	12.30
Secretary	11.82	10.35	10.50	10.37
Custodian	16.07	10.33	10.49	10.86

* The average compensation includes base salary, housing or parsonage allowance, retirement contribution, life and health insurance payments, and educational funds.

Table 4-12: Denominational Compensation Comparisons*

	Pastor	As. Pastor	CE Dir.	Youth	Choir	Admin.	Book.	Sec.	Custodian
A/G (517) **	80,913	62,926	51,415	52,359	60,718	52,509	31,309	27,869	35,178
Baptist (460)	73,352	63,471	57,084	50,431	63,100	57,735	32,158	25,497	29,755
Brethren (388)	73,707								
Catholic (632)								26,418	
Christian (354)	62,967	42,961						23,540	
CMA (611)	74,474	58,388		53,875					
Ch of Christ (423)								26,037	
Ch of God (507)	62,270	53,401		49,899				32,569	
Evang. Free (430)	82,159	69,861		60,894	66,784	52,843		28,574	33,585
Episcopal (586)	118,326	93,920		48,205	68,939	63,188		28,387	33,228
Independent (408)	73,582	62,675	54,845	54,749	60,470	52,445		29,929	33,815
Lutheran (386)	85,417	69,704	57,129	49,391	56,552	44,662		25,635	29,645
Nazarene (280)	58,495							22,535	
Nondenom. (474)	74,335	62,315	49,733	49,531	60,326	54,995	34,266	26,480	31,627
Presbyterian (378)	92,617	69,115	46,413	49,443	64,334	50,818	39,198	30,030	30,524
UCC (173)	67,398							26,315	
United Meth. (367)	81,031	57,372	36,986	38,977	45,567	37,059	27,196	25,844	24,651
Other*** (113)	72,788	63,280	49,784	49,904	56,333	53,409	33,169	26,505	33,621
National Average	77,096	64,034	51,983	50,371	60,316	53,153	33,336	26,624	31,026

* The average compensation includes base salary (including auto allowance), housing or parsonage allowance, retirement contribution, life and health insurance payments, and educational funds.

** The first number in parentheses following the denominational listing indicates the number of senior pastors reporting from that denomination. The second number is the average Sunday morning worship attendance for that denominational group. Blank spaces in the columns for other staff members indicates less than 10 respondents. Refer to "Other" at the bottom of the table.

*** Includes all other denominations with less than 10 respondents.

Chapter 5

Senior Pastors

Employment Profile

Senior pastors provided a significant number of responses to this survey with 900 participants. This group was composed of both pastors who oversee a multiple staff including other clergy and individual pastors who are the only ordained employee of their church. As can be expected, this group is quite diverse. Significant differences exist in training, church size, church income, and years served. Approximately 97% of the pastors surveyed serve full-time. The following statistical features profile this sample:

	Full-time	Part-time
Number of Respondents	870	30
Ordained	94%	86%
Average years employed	10	5
Male	96%	90%
Female	4%	10%
Self-employed	6%	18%
Church Employee	94%	72%
Senior pastor of multiple staff	81%	40%
Solo pastor	19%	60%
High School Diploma	5%	15%
Associate Degree	2%	4%
Bachelor Degree	23%	30%
Master Degree	42%	26%
Doctorate	28%	25%

Compensation Analysis

The analysis below is based upon the tables found later in this chapter. The tables present compensation data for pastors who serve full-time according to church attendance, church income, combinations of size and setting, gender, education, and years employed. The final table provides data for part-time pastors based upon the number of hours worked. In this way, the pastor's compensation can be analyzed and compared from a variety of useful perspectives. The total compensation amount includes the base salary, housing or parsonage amount, retirement contribution, life and health insurance payments, and educational funds.

Key Points

✎ Church income has the strongest correlation with compensation. While, the correlation is a fairly strong one, it should be considered as only one of many factors that determined compensation. In general, as church income increases, compensation goes up. In most years, pastors in churches with budgets over $600,000 tend to be equal to or above the national average compensation. Pastors serving churches with incomes over $1,000,000 receive on average over twice the compensation of a pastor in a church with a budget under $250,000. *See Table 5-2.*

✎ Church attendance affects pastoral compensation. Of the pastors surveyed, approximately 50% worked in churches with an average attendance under 300 people. The compensation of these pastors was below the national average. Compensation increases significantly as attendance moves between 200 to 300. The average number of years served tends to increase as attendance increases. *See Table 5-1.*

✎ A church's geographical setting affects pastoral compensation. Generally, pastors of suburban and urban churches have the highest compensation. Historically, urban pastors have the highest levels of compensation for larger churches. Churches located in urban, suburban and medium size cities tend to provide higher housing allowances, retirement contributions, and insurance payments, although health insurance payments are often comparable. *See Tables 5-3, 5-4, 5-5, 5-6 and 5-7.*

✎ Gender disparities exist concerning pastoral compensation. On average, female pastors earn less than their male counterparts, but the gap has declined somewhat over the past decade. At this time, women do not have access to larger churches. The average congregational size that men serve is about 450 people, while for women it is under 200. The difference in congregational size represents a considerable difference in church income which impacts the overall compensation. *See Table 5-8.*

✎ A relationship exists between educational achievement and income for pastors. Pastors with a high school diploma earned approximately $13,700 less than pastors with a master's degree. In general, only those groups with graduate degrees reached the national average. A significant increase in compensation occurs for pastors with a doctoral degree. These individuals are more likely to serve larger urban or suburban churches which provide the highest levels of compensation. Average years employed tends to be similar regardless of educational background. Over 90% of the respondents were college graduates and 71% had graduate degrees. The most common was a master's degree held by 42% of those responding to this survey. Over 28% held doctoral degrees. *See Table 5-9.*

✎ Years of service has an impact on compensation. Those serving for less than five years in their current position (36% of the respondents) received about $14,300 a year less in total compensation than those who had served over 15 years. The difference, however, appears to be more dependent on church income than on years served. Those serving the longest tended to be in bigger churches with significantly higher incomes. *See Table 5-10.*

✎ On average, part-time pastors work 23 hours per week for their church. Most part-time pastors serve churches with an average attendance of 100 people. Their tenure is shorter than that of full-time pastors. Comparatively, compensation is significantly less for part-time pastors than those serving full-time. *See Table 5-11.*

Benefit Analysis

Full-time staff members. The pastor was the most highly paid position in the local church and received the best benefits. Most pastors own or rent a home. Slightly over three-fourths of pastors received health insurance and 67% had retirement benefits.

Part-time staff members. Approximately 3% of the pastors in this survey served their church on a part-time basis. Part-time pastors received fewer benefits than full-time pastors in every compensation category.

Benefits	Full-time	Part-time
☐ Housing allowance	82%	53%
☐ Parsonage provided	15%	27%
☐ Retirement	67%	13%
☐ Health insurance	79%	20%
☐ Life insurance	36%	3%
☐ Paid vacation	93%	57%
☐ Auto allowance	85%	37%
☐ Continuing education expenses	45%	30%

Ten Year Compensation Trend: National Averages for Pastors

1996: $55,027	2001: $69,543
1997: $56,172	2002: $71,232
1998: $59,067	2003: $73,230
1999: $62,869	2004: $74,969
2000: $66,096	2005: $77,096

Table 5-1: Annual Compensation Of Senior Pastor By Worship Attendance

Church Attendance	0-99	100-299	300-499	500-749	750-999	1,000+
Number Of Respondents	134	310	165	96	55	94
Salary (98%)	27,255	37,056	43,837	50,027	58,703	67,844
Annual % Increase (67%)	5%	5%	4%	4%	5%	6%
Parsonage (15%)	10,409	13,865	15,584	25,898	19,125	26,943
Housing (82%)	15,128	20,263	25,372	29,303	29,588	37,537
Retirement (67%)	4,051	5,028	5,755	7,260	7,872	6,307
Life Insurance (36%)	749	816,	552	669	1,046	813
Health Insurance (79%)	6,487	8,871	9,860	10,452	11,665	9,480
Vacation/weeks (93%)	3	4	4	4	4	4
Education Funds (45%)	1,166	1,259	1,905	1,653	1,824	1,879
Receive Auto Allow. (85%)	73%	81%	90%	93%	95%	90%

* The percentage following each compensation item indicates the portion of all senior pastors who received that form of compensation. The averages in each column are for those individuals who actually received that compensation item. See Chapter 3 for a full explanation of how to read this table.

Total Compensation Comparisons

Church Attendance	0-99	100-299	300-499	500-749	750-999	1,000+
Average attendance	64	180	374	587	883	1,612
Average church income	127,035	359,637	752,429	1,285,835	1,595,145	2,887,580
Average years employed	7	8	10	16	13	15
Average compensation*	46,509	66,461	81,407	94,398	102,334	115,577
Standard deviation	18,165	22,102	22,035	24,151	25,710	35,964
Median compensation	44,200	64,164	79,598	91,650	101,772	111,000

National average: $77,096 with a standard deviation of $31,588 (see Chapter 4, Table 4-3).

Total respondents: 854

* includes base salary, housing or parsonage allowance, retirement contribution, life and health insurance payments, and educational funds.

Table 5-2: Annual Compensation Of Senior Pastor By Church Income

Church Income in $	0-249,999	250,000-499,999	500,000-749,000	750,000-999,999	1,000,000 +
Number Of Respondents	232	157	140	66	223
Salary (98%)	30,440	36,141	42,718	45,776	59,258
Annual % Increase (67%)	6%	4%	5%	4%	5%
Parsonage (15%)	11,121	12,676	17,369	17,673	25,950
Housing (82%)	15,243	22,469	24,414	26,019	33,654
Retirement (67%)	4,036	5,162	5,570	6,995	7,154
Life Insurance (36%)	803	828	596	868	810
Health Insurance (79%)	7,295	8,560	9,885	10,254	10,567
Vacation/weeks (93%)	3	4	4	4	4
Education Funds (45%)	1,182	1,508	1,623	1,640	1,785
Receive Auto Allow. (85%)	78%	81%	84%	91%	94%

* The percentage following each compensation item indicates the portion of all senior pastors who received that form of compensation. The averages in each column are for those individuals who actually received that compensation item. See Chapter 3 for a full explanation of how to read this table.

Total Compensation Comparisons

Church Income	0-249,999	250,000-499,999	500,000-749,999	750,000-999,999	1,000,000+
Average attendance	114	212	363	420	997
Average church income	147,113	349,040	605,745	855,158	2,133,227
Average years employed	7	9	10	11	13
Average compensation*	52,362	67,420	77,915	85,669	106,337
Standard deviation	21,243	18,855	22,043	22,427	30,546
Median compensation	51,100	65,992	76,175	83,696	103,000

National average: $77,096 with a standard deviation of $31,588 (see Chapter 4, Table 4-3).

Total respondents: 818

* includes base salary, housing or parsonage allowance, retirement contribution, life and health insurance payments, and educational funds.

Table 5-3: Annual Compensation Of Senior Pastor By Church Setting And Size

Attendance 0-250	Urban	Suburban	Medium City	Small Town	Rural
Number Of Respondents	46	112	77	127	58
Salary (98%)	37,746	37,320	35,317	30,251	29,950
Annual % Increase (67%)	6%	5%	5%	5%	4%
Parsonage (15%)	16,264	17,319	17,049	9,542	6,647
Housing (82%)	20,343	21,552	19,443	17,012	12,519
Retirement (67%)	5,721	5,976	4,932	3,875	3,804
Life Insurance (36%)	414	986	1,034	751	753
Health Insurance (79%)	9,506	9,001	7,770	7,716	6,360
Vacation/weeks (93%)	4	4	4	3	3
Education Funds (45%)	1,399	1,233	1,574	1,124	1,015
Receive Auto Allow. (85%)	83%	84%	78%	74%	76%

* The percentage following each compensation item indicates the portion of all senior pastors who received that form of compensation. The averages in each column are for those individuals who actually received that compensation item. See Chapter 3 for a full explanation of how to read this table.

Total Compensation Comparisons

Church Size: 0-250	Urban	Suburban	Medium City	Small Town	Rural
Average attendance	129	147	152	121	116
Average church income	408,897	345,422	329,730	227,764	176,005
Average years employed	8	8	10	8	8
Average compensation*	68,353	68,280	62,581	53,619	47,861
Standard deviation	29,314	23,089	25,063	17,691	18,438
Median compensation	63,592	68,730	59,500	52,640	45,892

National average: $77,096 with a standard deviation of $31,588 (see Chapter 4, Table 4-3).

Total respondents: 420

* includes base salary, housing or parsonage allowance, retirement contribution, life and health insurance payments, and educational funds.

Table 5-4: Annual Compensation Of Senior Pastor By Church Setting And Size

Attendance 251-500	Urban	Suburban	Medium City	Small Town	Rural
Number Of Respondents	23	79	53	53	7
Salary (98%)	43,155	44,721	41,991	40,323	41,239
Annual % Increase (67%)	4%	4%	5%	4%	5%
Parsonage (15%)	17,088	19,560	19,850	6,777	14,667
Housing (82%)	32,038	29,507	24,782	21,533	27,583
Retirement (67%)	7,561	5,490	5,794	4,908	4,589
Life Insurance (36%)	872	556	476	639	206
Health Insurance (79%)	9,104	10,838	10,436	8,750	6,545
Vacation/weeks (93%)	4	4	4	4	4
Education Funds (45%)	1,902	1,659	1,854	2,441	1,733
Receive Auto Allow. (85%)	100%	91%	87%	85%	100%

* The percentage following each compensation item indicates the portion of all senior pastors who received that form of compensation. The averages in each column are for those individuals who actually received that compensation item. See Chapter 3 for a full explanation of how to read this table.

Total Compensation Comparisons

Church Size: 251-500	Urban	Suburban	Medium City	Small Town	Rural
Average attendance	339	368	389	366	336
Average church income	861,377	738,537	723,091	674,542	600,233
Average years employed	10	10	10	9	9
Average compensation*	87,887	86,475	77,980	72,578	80,607
Standard deviation	28,430	22,375	20,632	19,497	25,142
Median compensation	83,696	83,174	76,773	73,000	66,075

National average: $77,096 with a standard deviation of $31,588 (see Chapter 4, Table 4-3).

Total respondents: 215

* includes base salary, housing or parsonage allowance, retirement contribution, life and health insurance payments, and educational funds.

Table 5-5: Annual Compensation Of Senior Pastor By Church Setting And Size

Attendance 501-750	Urban	Suburban	Medium City	Small Town	Rural
Number Of Respondents	12	36	27	10	4
Salary (98%)	64,664	51,098	46,872	56,530	45,798
Annual % Increase (67%)	4%	4%	3%	4%	4%
Parsonage (15%)	39,230	15,000	9,360	0	0
Housing (82%)	30,887	31,320	29,044	18,789	14,752
Retirement (67%)	11,875	6,037	5,745	7,253	11,340
Life Insurance (36%)	460	897	544	325	2,484
Health Insurance (79%)	9,533	11,874	9,643	12,390	7,059
Vacation/weeks (93%)	4	4	4	4	4
Education Funds (45%)	2,071	1,552	1,231	1,150	800
Receive Auto Allow. (85%)	92%	92%	100%	100%	100%

* The percentage following each compensation item indicates the portion of all senior pastors who received that form of compensation. The averages in each column are for those individuals who actually received that compensation item. See Chapter 3 for a full explanation of how to read this table.

Total Compensation Comparisons

Church Size: 501-750	Urban	Suburban	Medium City	Small Town	Rural
Average attendance	615	631	641	612	596
Average church income	2,266,476	1,220,766	1,198,905	1,077,222	764,211
Average years employed	10	14	13	13	16
Average compensation*	116,357	94,965	88,294	93,128	80,991
Standard deviation	33,124	18,872	19,842	15,410	20,487
Median compensation	111,066	92,328	84,305	89,650	70,720

National average: $77,096 with a standard deviation of $31,588 (see Chapter 4, Table 4-3).

Total respondents: 89

* includes base salary, housing or parsonage allowance, retirement contribution, life and health insurance payments, and educational funds.

Table 5-6: Annual Compensation Of Senior Pastor By Church Setting And Size

Attendance 751-1,000	Urban	Suburban	Medium City	Small Town	Rural
Number Of Respondents	10	23	11	7	2
Salary (98%)	61,563	67,968	56,046	52,869	49,088
Annual % Increase (67%)	4%	5%	4%	6%	4%
Parsonage (15%)	21,400	18,000	15,250	28,000	0
Housing (82%)	39,626	34,975	27,552	24,309	15,000
Retirement (67%)	10,382	7,822	5,464	8,079	1,843
Life Insurance (36%)	461	1,542	436	1,382	168
Health Insurance (79%)	11,202	10,713	10,993	10,348	8,276
Vacation/weeks (93%)	4	4	4	4	4
Education Funds (45%)	2,383	2,033	1,624	1,200	1,000
Receive Auto Allow. (85%)	90%	91%	100%	86%	100%

* The percentage following each compensation item indicates the portion of all senior pastors who received that form of compensation. The averages in each column are for those individuals who actually received that compensation item. See Chapter 3 for a full explanation of how to read this table.

Total Compensation Comparisons

Church Size: 751-1000	Urban	Suburban	Medium Town	Small Town	Rural
Average attendance	918	895	884	875	790
Average church income	1,926,280	2,138,947	1,589,526	1,349,735	1,416,538
Average years employed	16	10	14	14	20
Average compensation*	108,304	114,148	97,756	97,711	69,732
Standard deviation	46,017	20,341	24,814	21,477	8,157
Median compensation	116,394	110,387	85,578	84,240	n/a

National average: $77,096 with a standard deviation of $31,588 (see Chapter 4, Table 4-3).

Total respondents: 53

* includes base salary, housing or parsonage allowance, retirement contribution, life and health insurance payments, and educational funds.

Table 5-7: Annual Compensation Of Senior Pastor By Church Setting And Size

Attendance Over 1,000	Urban	Suburban	Medium City	Small Town	Rural
Number Of Respondents	8	36	31	4	0
Salary (98%)	61,289	66,961	69,103	73,721	
Annual % Increase (67%)	5%	6%	5%	9%	
Parsonage (15%)	0	29,267	17,460	0	
Housing (82%)	37,684	42,597	35,094	23,646	
Retirement (67%)	8,450	6,645	5,862	5,064	
Life Insurance (36%)	947	962	515	928	
Health Insurance (79%)	11,415	10,384	8,919	6,247	
Vacation/weeks (93%)	4	4	4	3	
Education Funds (45%)	650	1,787	1,970	2,000	
Receive Auto Allow. (85%)	88%	94%	90%	75%	

* The percentage following each compensation item indicates the portion of all senior pastors who received that form of compensation. The averages in each column are for those individuals who actually received that compensation item. See Chapter 3 for a full explanation of how to read this table.

Total Compensation Comparisons

Church Size: 1,000 +	Urban	Suburban	Medium City	Small Town	Rural
Average attendance	1,833	1,783	1,644	1,225	
Average church income	3,445,193	3,244,300	2,625,474	2,584,787	
Average years employed	10	15	16	22	
Average compensation*	108,796	122,692	114,503	105,779	
Standard deviation	27,994	37,603	27,504	43,373	
Median compensation	102,900	114,962	104,655	101,253	

National average: $77,096 with a standard deviation of $31,588 (see Chapter 4, Table 4-3).

Total respondents: 79

* includes base salary, housing or parsonage allowance, retirement contribution, life and health insurance payments, and educational funds.

Table 5-8: Annual Compensation Of Senior Pastor By Gender

Gender	Male	Female
Number Of Respondents	836	31
Salary (98%)	43,363	32,657
Annual % Increase (67%)	5%	5%
Parsonage (15%)	14,537	11,175
Housing (82%)	24,672	19,940
Retirement (67%)	5,711	6,127
Life Insurance (36%)	763	598
Health Insurance (79%)	9,267	8,204
Vacation/weeks (93%)	4	4
Education Funds (45%)	1,543	1,324
Receive Auto Allow. (85%)	86%	71%

* The percentage following each compensation item indicates the portion of all senior pastors who received that form of compensation. The averages in each column are for those individuals who actually received that compensation item. See Chapter 3 for a full explanation of how to read this table.

Total Compensation Comparisons

Gender	Male	Female
Average attendance	454	170
Average church income	880,141	330,038
Average years employed	10	6
Average compensation*	77,550	62,690
Standard deviation	31,578	24,670
Median compensation	74,174	61,732

National average: $77,096 with a standard deviation of $31,588 (see Chapter 4, Table 4-3).

Total respondents: 867

* includes base salary, housing or parsonage allowance, retirement contribution, life and health insurance payments, and educational funds.

Table 5-9: Annual Compensation Of Senior Pastor By Education

Highest Degree	High School	Associate	Bachelor	Master	Doctorate
Number Of Respondents	41	12	178	334	224
Salary (98%)	35,034	26,716	37,973	43,044	49,347
Annual % Increase (67%)	6%	7%	5%	5%	5%
Parsonage (15%)	10,979	17,321	10,758	13,302	20,507
Housing (82%)	27,306	21,458	22,467	23,893	26,798
Retirement (67%)	5,731	3,028	4,151	5,562	7,031
Life Insurance (36%)	710	0	830	711	814
Health Insurance (79%)	6,581	5,300	8,681	9,259	10,288
Vacation/weeks (93%)	3	3	4	4	4
Education Funds (45%)	1,600	1,250	1,442	1,523	1,661
Receive Auto Allow. (85%)	85%	75%	84%	84%	91%

* The percentage following each compensation item indicates the portion of all senior pastors who received that form of compensation. The averages in each column are for those individuals who actually received that compensation item. See Chapter 3 for a full explanation of how to read this table.

Total Compensation Comparisons

Highest Degree	High School	Associate	Bachelor	Masters	Doctorate
Average attendance	453	146	352	453	548
Average church income	807,840	256,609	622,752	841,186	1,166,938
Average years employed	12	9	11	10	11
Average compensation*	63,625	49,471	67,411	77,341	89,217
Standard deviation	42,598	27,920	28,190	29,904	30,181
Median compensation	49,035	40,700	63,708	73,083	88,015

National average: $77,096 with a standard deviation of $31,588 (see Chapter 4, Table 4-3).

Total respondents: 789

* includes base salary, housing or parsonage allowance, retirement contribution, life and health insurance payments, and educational funds.

Table 5-10: Annual Compensation Of Senior Pastor By Years Employed

Years Employed	0-5	6-10	11-15	over 15
Number Of Respondents	343	190	130	194
Salary (98%)	39,354	41,459	47,266	48,224
Annual % Increase (67%)	5%	5%	5%	4%
Parsonage (15%)	12,946	13,366	19,105	17,034
Housing (82%)	22,595	23,324	28,222	26,535
Retirement (67%)	5,562	5,784	5,108	6,319
Life Insurance (36%)	722	735	726	858
Health Insurance (79%)	9,358	8,509	9,245	9,710
Vacation/weeks (93%)	3	3	4	4
Education Funds (45%)	1,541	1,466	1,724	1,450
Receive Auto Allow. (85%)	83%	86%	88%	88%

* The percentage following each compensation item indicates the portion of all senior pastors who received that form of compensation. The averages in each column are for those individuals who actually received that compensation item. See Chapter 3 for a full explanation of how to read this table.

Total Compensation Comparisons

Years Employed	0-5	6-10	11-15	Over 15
Average attendance	310	402	566	638
Average church income	617,235	775,015	1,235,843	1,146,817
Average years employed	3	8	13	23
Average compensation*	71,107	74,184	85,240	85,386
Standard deviation	28,160	31,141	35,964	31,521
Median compensation	66,785	69,779	81,641	81,800

National average: $77,096 with a standard deviation of $31,588 (see Chapter 4, Table 4-3).

Total respondents: 857

* includes base salary, housing or parsonage allowance, retirement contribution, life and health insurance payments, and educational funds.

Table 5-11: Annual Compensation Of Part-Time Senior Pastors By Hours Worked

Hours Per Week	1-14	15-29	30-39	All Part-time
Number of Respondents	2	3	4	30
Salary (83%)	11,200	52,246	18,458	21,201
Annual % Increase (37%)	3%	6%	2%	4%
Parsonage (27%)	0	3,000	0	10,420
Housing (53%)	780	3,000	16,000	14,480
Retirement (13%)	0	0	2,290	9,222
Life Insurance (3%)	0	1,500	0	1,500
Health Insurance (20%)	0	0	5,685	6,734
Vacation/weeks (57%)	2	4	2	3
Education Funds (30%)	0	0	2,000	878
Receive Auto Allow. (37%)	100%	67%	100%	37%

* The percentage following each compensation item indicates the portion of all part-time senior pastors who received that form of compensation. The averages in each column are for those individuals who actually received that compensation item. See Chapter 3 for a full explanation of how to read this table.

Total Compensation Comparisons

Hours Per Week	1-14	15-29	30-39	All Part-time
Average attendance	95	263	78	99
Average church income	229,500	488,924	299,514	202,895
Average years employed	1	11	4	5
Average hours per week	8	20	33	23
Average compensation	11,590	55,996	34,374	33,277
Ave. hourly compensation*	27.86	53.84	20.03	27.82
Ave. hourly salary**	26.92	50.24	10.76	16.89

Total respondents: 30

* includes base salary, housing or parsonage allowance, retirement contribution, life and health insurance payments, and educational funds (note: auto allowance is included in base salary).

** includes base salary only; see discussion on "rounding errors" in Chapter 3.

Chapter 6

Associate Pastors

Employment Profile

The roles and duties of the associate pastor are quite diverse depending upon the church. Associate pastors receive approximately the same benefits as senior pastors, but the total compensation amounts are considerably less. On average, associate pastors tend to receive a compensation of about 75-85% of that of pastors. The gap widens even more once church attendance exceeds 1,000 or church income passes $1,000,000. The statistical profile of associate pastors was as follows:

	Full-time	Part-time
❏ Number of Respondents	405	68
❏ Ordained	87%	85%
❏ Male	90%	79%
❏ Female	10%	21%
❏ Years employed	7	5
❏ Self-employed	4%	5%
❏ Church Employee	96%	95%
❏ High School Diploma	7%	11%
❏ Associate Degree	2%	4%
❏ Bachelor Degree	31%	31%
❏ Master Degree	50%	43%
❏ Doctorate	10%	11%

Compensation Analysis

The analysis below is based upon the tables found later in this chapter. The tables present compensation data for associate pastors who serve full-time according to worship attendance, church income, combinations of size and setting, gender, education, and years employed. The final table provides data for part-time pastors based upon the number of hours worked. In this way, the associate pastor's compensation can be analyzed and compared from a variety of useful perspectives. The total compensation amount includes the base salary, housing or parsonage allowance, retirement contribution, life and health insurance payments, and educational funds.

Key Points

✎ *Church worship attendance has a direct influence upon the compensation of the associate pastor.* In general, associate pastors in churches with an average attendance under 500 aree below the national average; others aree above. The value of several fringe benefits also tends to increase with church size. *See Table 6-1.*

✎ *Church income impacts the compensation of associate pastors.* Church income is the most important factor affecting total compensation, although many factors play a role. About 50% of the associate pastors served in churches with an average annual budget over $1,000,000. Housing allowance amount increased with church income. Total compensation did not reach the national average until the church's annual income reached approached $900,000 per year. *See Table 6-2.*

✎ *A church's geographic setting impacts the compensation of associate pastors.* In general, associate pastors serving churches located in suburban, urban and medium size cities receive the highest average compensation. Generally, urban churches tend to have the highest church income. Typically, individuals serving in rural churches receive the lowest average compensation. *See Tables 6-3, 6-4, 6-5, 6-6, and 6-7.*

✎ *Female associate pastors receive lower levels of compensation than did their male counterparts.* On average, females earned 75% of the compensation of their male counterparts, down from 88% last year, and 92% two years ago. Men tend to serve in much larger churches with budgets averaging far more than those churches in which females serve. That church income difference may account for part of the compensation differential. *See Table 6-8.*

✎ *College graduates earn more than nongraduates, but the highest compensation levels are found with those having graduate degrees.* Sixty percent of this sample had graduate degrees. These individuals received higher levels of compensations than those with less education. They tend to work in urban or suburban churches which generally have significantly higher levels of income than other churches. Associate pastors with a bachelor's degree earned significantly more than those with a high school diploma (although that gap differs widely from one year to the next). Both, however, were below the national average. *See Table 6-9.*

✎ *Total compensation is partially tied to length of service.* Compensation tends to increase with length of service. Those serving the longest tend to serve in churches with average annual incomes in the 1.4 to 2 million dollar range. In general, church income is more significant than years served on final compensation amounts, although, in this sample, those with 21 years of service earned significantly more than those with under 5 years of service, but not much more than those serving at least 10 years. *See Table 6-10.*

✎ *Most part-time associate pastors work about half-time at the church.* The average annual compensation for these part-time associates is significantly lower than their full-time counterparts. *See Table 6-11.*

Benefit Analysis

Full-time staff members. Full-time associate pastors received benefit packages commensurate with those of senior pastors. Senior pastors were more likely to live in a church owned parsonage than were associates, although about the same percentage from both groups had a housing allowance as part of their compensation. For a comparative analysis of all staff positions, see Table 4-1 in Chapter 4.

Part-time staff members. About 14% percent of the associate pastors participating in this survey worked at their church on a part-time basis. Salary and benefits were tied to the number of hours employed.

Benefits	**Full-time**	**Part-time**
❏ Housing allowance	81%	57%
❏ Parsonage provided	7%	4%
❏ Retirement contributions	62%	7%
❏ Life insurance	41%	9%
❏ Health insurance	79%	26%
❏ Paid vacation	95%	57%
❏ Auto allowance	87%	81%
❏ Continuing education funds	44%	32%

Ten Year Compensation Trend: National Averages for Associate Pastors

❏	1996	$44,710
❏	1997	$45,042
❏	1998	$47,076
❏	1999	$49,827
❏	2000	$51,973
❏	2001	$54,729
❏	2002	$58,072
❏	2003	$59,742
❏	2004	$61,263
❏	2005	$64,034

Table 6-1: Annual Compensation Of Associate Pastor By Worship Attendance

Church Attendance	0-99	100-299	300-499	500-749	750-999	1,000+
Number Of Respondents	4	84	99	83	49	79
Salary (99%*)	23,290	28,119	31,086	35,159	36,957	46,072
Annual % Increase (73%)	15%	5%	5%	4%	4%	5%
Parsonage (7%)	0	10,389	16,138	11,600	11,183	21,204
Housing (81%)	9,000	16,463	20,172	23,731	21,917	27,414
Retirement (62%)	2,250	3,141	3,935	4,411	5,513	4,296
Life Insurance (41%)	408	751	357	355	618	371
Health Insurance (79%)	9,234	7,852	8,700	9,854	10,586	8,351
Vacation/weeks (95%)	4	3	3	4	4	4
Education Fund (44%)	2,000	1,217	1,245	1,223	1,531	1,432
Receive Auto Allow. (87%)	100%	74%	87%	92%	94%	91%

* The percentage following each compensation item indicates the portion of all associate pastors who received that form of compensation. The averages in each column are for those individuals who actually received that compensation item. See Chapter 3 for a full explanation of how to read this table.

Total Compensation Comparisons

Church Attendance	0-99	100-299	300-499	500-749	750-999	Over 1,000
Average attendance	73	207	377	593	833	1,651
Average church income	171,745	448,565	809,802	1,363,445	1,610,248	2,943,290
Average years employed	11	5	6	8	7	9
Annual compensation*	31,986	49,430	58,280	67,806	68,402	82,016
Standard deviation	15,754	16,866	16,709	17,390	21,345	39,734
Median compensation	23,660	48,100	58,329	68,575	66,299	74,907

National average: $64,034 with a standard deviation of $26,369 (see Chapter 4, Table 4-3).

Total respondents: 398

* includes base salary, housing or parsonage allowance, retirement contribution, life and health insurance payments, and educational funds.

Table 6-2: Annual Compensation Of Associate Pastor By Church Income

Church Income in $	0-249,999	250,000-499,999	500,000-749,000	750,000-999,999	1,000,000 +
Number Of Respondents	23	49	69	46	192
Salary (99%*)	27,139	25,524	32,315	30,955	39,403
Annual % Increase (73%)	8%	5%	5%	4%	5%
Parsonage (7%)	18,600	10,725	11,504	11,669	17,681
Housing (81%)	13,102	17,567	18,124	20,113	25,703
Retirement (62%)	2,713	3,810	3,485	3,386	4,868
Life Insurance (41%)	324	935	427	251	417
Health Insurance (79%)	8,291	7,934	9,248	8,428	9,169
Vacation/weeks (95%)	3	3	3	3	4
Education Fund (44%)	1,796	982	1,093	1,461	1,364
Receive Auto Allow. (87%)	74%	82%	75%	87%	94%

* The percentage following each compensation item indicates the portion of all associate pastors who received that form of compensation. The averages in each column are for those individuals who actually received that compensation item. See Chapter 3 for a full explanation of how to read this table.

Total Compensation Comparisons

Church Budget	0-249,999	250,000-499,999	500,000-749,999	750,000-999,999	Over 1,000,000
Average attendance	263	235	393	428	1,019
Average church income	184,747	367,137	618,848	855,816	2,169,364
Average years employed	6	5	8	5	8
Annual compensation*	43,758	48,778	57,832	57,461	73,647
Standard deviation	19,395	15,768	17,676	14,866	29,936
Median compensation	35,520	47,000	59,813	56,753	70,400

National average: $64,034 with a standard deviation of $26,369 (see Chapter 4, Table 4-3).

Total respondents: 379

* includes base salary, housing or parsonage allowance, retirement contribution, life and health insurance payments, and educational funds.

Table 6-3: Annual Compensation Of Associate Pastor By Church Setting And Size

Attendance 0-250	Urban	Suburban	Medium City	Small Town	Rural
Number Of Respondents	13	21	16	20	6
Salary (99%*)	29,368	23,729	30,672	26,681	28,596
Annual % Increase (73%)	9%	5%	6%	5%	4%
Parsonage (7%)	0	12,875	7,200	11,700	0
Housing (81%)	18,636	18,789	14,919	14,207	11,968
Retirement (62%)	5,468	2,836	2,750	2,630	3,375
Life Insurance (41%)	408	231	860	2,382	965
Health Insurance (79%)	7,602	8,942	9,254	7,003	6,588
Vacation/weeks (95%)	3	3	3	3	3
Education Fund (44%)	1,517	1,039	1,600	1,000	1,233
Receive Auto Allow. (87%)	85%	76%	75%	65%	100%

* The percentage following each compensation item indicates the portion of all associate pastors who received that form of compensation. The averages in each column are for those individuals who actually received that compensation item. See Chapter 3 for a full explanation of how to read this table.

Total Compensation Comparisons

Church Size: 0-250	Urban	Suburban	Medium City	Small Town	Rural
Average attendance	147	194	206	163	222
Average church income	643,503	558,806	459,831	395,095	272,228
Average years employed	6	4	4	7	5
Annual compensation*	53,526	50,362	47,225	46,554	45,052
Standard deviation	32,726	17,755	19,533	14,171	15,054
Median compensation	38,400	52,396	45,270	43,329	45,251

National average: $64,034 with a standard deviation of $26,369 (see Chapter 4, Table 4-3).

Total respondents: 76

* includes base salary, housing or parsonage allowance, retirement contribution, life and health insurance payments, and educational funds.

Table 6-4: Annual Compensation Of Associate Pastor By Church Setting And Size

Attendance 251-500	Urban	Suburban	Medium City	Small Town	Rural
Number Of Respondents	14	51	31	30	0
Salary (99%*)	29,820	31,684	32,624	31,177	
Annual % Increase (73%)	5%	4%	5%	5%	
Parsonage (7%)	0	14,158	5,000	0	
Housing (81%)	22,483	21,990	17,537	19,825	
Retirement (62%)	4,280	3,915	3,485	4,556	
Life Insurance (41%)	172	315	439	358	
Health Insurance (79%)	6,606	8,941	8,594	8,898	
Vacation/weeks (95%)	3	3	4	3	
Education Fund (44%)	881	1,109	1,519	1,521	
Receive Auto Allow. (87%)	93%	88%	81%	80%	

* The percentage following each compensation item indicates the portion of all associate pastors who received that form of compensation. The averages in each column are for those individuals who actually received that compensation item. See Chapter 3 for a full explanation of how to read this table.

Total Compensation Comparisons

Church Size: 251-500	Urban	Suburban	Medium City	Small Town	Rural
Average attendance	332	378	398	378	
Average church income	916,961	788,199	743,296	780,472	
Average years employed	7	5	7	9	
Annual compensation*	54,426	58,546	60,061	57,778	
Standard deviation	13,050	18,511	14,299	15,997	
Median compensation	49,950	61,004	58,360	56,937	

National average: $64,034 with a standard deviation of $26,369 (see Chapter 4, Table 4-3).

Total respondents: 126

* includes base salary, housing or parsonage allowance, retirement contribution, life and health insurance payments, and educational funds.

Table 6-5: Annual Compensation Of Associate Pastor By Church Setting And Size

Attendance 501-750	Urban	Suburban	Medium City	Small Town	Rural
Number Of Respondents	10	31	24	9	3
Salary (99%*)	37,529	35,743	29,602	36,702	35,225
Annual % Increase (73%)	3%	4%	5%	4%	3%
Parsonage (7%)	0	14,400	0	0	6,000
Housing (81%)	24,526	24,037	26,951	14,988	11,138
Retirement (62%)	6,887	4,872	3,560	2,876	1,306
Life Insurance (41%)	360	577	188	210	48
Health Insurance (79%)	10,176	11,086	9,032	9,018	10,443
Vacation/weeks (95%)	4	4	4	3	4
Education Fund (44%)	1,562	1,279	954	563	1,067
Receive Auto Allow. (87%)	100%	90%	100%	89%	100%

* The percentage following each compensation item indicates the portion of all associate pastors who received that form of compensation. The averages in each column are for those individuals who actually received that compensation item. See Chapter 3 for a full explanation of how to read this table.

Total Compensation Comparisons

Church Size: 0501-750	Urban	Suburban	Medium City	Small Town	Rural
Average attendance	620	633	638	613	619
Average church income	2,411,046	1,283,673	1,253,032	1,105,625	720,948
Average years employed	8	9	8	7	9
Annual compensation*	75,095	69,467	66,552	59,300	57,481
Standard deviation	9,680	18,258	14,113	18,947	14,585
Median compensation	71,400	63,588	65,939	52,718	41,665

National average: $64,034 with a standard deviation of $26,369 (see Chapter 4, Table 4-3).

Total respondents: 77

* includes base salary, housing or parsonage allowance, retirement contribution, life and health insurance payments, and educational funds.

Table 6-6: Annual Compensation Of Associate Pastor By Church Setting And Size

Attendance 751-1,000	Urban	Suburban	Medium City	Small Town	Rural
Number Of Respondents	8	21	9	7	0
Salary (99%*)	46,976	39,360	38,310	38,178	
Annual % Increase (73%)	3%	4%	4%	5%	
Parsonage (7%)	0	12,000	4,800	16,750	
Housing (81%)	26,675	24,012	20,528	18,264	
Retirement (62%)	9,020	4,599	3,515	4,996	
Life Insurance (41%)	607	860	308	1,200	
Health Insurance (79%)	9,446	9,899	10,481	9,732	
Vacation/weeks (95%)	4	3	4	4	
Education Fund (44%)	2,925	1,446	1,471	1,100	
Receive Auto Allow. (87%)	100%	90%	100%	86%	

* The percentage following each compensation item indicates the portion of all associate pastors who received that form of compensation. The averages in each column are for those individuals who actually received that compensation item. See Chapter 3 for a full explanation of how to read this table.

Total Compensation Comparisons

Church Size: 751-1000	Urban	Suburban	Medium City	Small Town	Rural
Average attendance	900	887	881	875	
Average church income	1,995,350	2,112,518	1,710,092	1,349,735	
Average years employed	13	5	9	7	
Annual compensation*	89,418	69,076	69,285	71,231	
Standard deviation	25,344	19,610	22,780	8,658	
Median compensation	75,060	69,897	64,384	66,440	

National average: $64,034 with a standard deviation of $26,369 (see Chapter 4, Table 4-3).

Total respondents: 45

* includes base salary, housing or parsonage allowance, retirement contribution, life and health insurance payments, and educational funds.

Table 6-7: Annual Compensation Of Associate Pastor By Church Setting And Size

Attendance Over 1,000	Urban	Suburban	Medium City	Small Town	Rural
Number Of Respondents	4	29	30	4	0
Salary (99%*)	42,578	44,831	40,400	60628	
Annual % Increase (73%)	4%	7%	5%	6%	
Parsonage (7%)	0	19,300	18,120	0	
Housing (81%)	30,300	31,529	25,643	17,334	
Retirement (62%)	7,581	5,594	3,408	2,198	
Life Insurance (41%)	459	284	292	383	
Health Insurance (79%)	8,810	9,446	7,830	6,889	
Vacation/weeks (95%)	4	4	4	2	
Education Fund (44%)	650	1,084	1,686	2,000	
Receive Auto Allow. (87%)	100%	93%	90%	75%	

* The percentage following each compensation item indicates the portion of all associate pastors who received that form of compensation. The averages in each column are for those individuals who actually received that compensation item. See Chapter 3 for a full explanation of how to read this table.

Total Compensation Comparisons

Church Size: 1,000 +	Urban	Suburban	Medium City	Small Town	Rural
Average attendance	2,138	1,839	1,658	1,225	
Average church income	2,750,000	3,472,636	2,713,939	2,584,787	
Average years employed	11	8	10	8	
Annual compensation*	87,651	87,491	72,789	89,771	
Standard deviation	32,078	23,235	18,638	42,175	
Median compensation	77,435	81,541	70,871	65,445	

National average: $64,034 with a standard deviation of $26,369 (see Chapter 4, Table 4-3).

Total respondents: 67

* includes base salary, housing or parsonage allowance, retirement contribution, life and health insurance payments, and educational funds.

Table 6-8: Annual Compensation Of Associate Pastor By Gender

Gender	Male	Female
Number Of Respondents	363	40
Salary (99%*)	35,120	32,280
Annual % Increase (73%)	5%	6%
Parsonage (7%)	14,685	6,000
Housing (81%)	22,279	17,142
Retirement (62%)	4,272	3,848
Life Insurance (41%)	428	431
Health Insurance (79%)	9,234	6,250
Vacation/weeks (95%)	3	3
Education Fund (44%)	1,297	1,372
Receive Auto Allow. (87%)	87%	93%

* The percentage following each compensation item indicates the portion of all associate pastors who received that form of compensation. The averages in each column are for those individuals who actually received that compensation item. See Chapter 3 for a full explanation of how to read this table.

Total Compensation Comparisons

Gender	Male	Female
Average attendance	716	466
Average church income	1,414,884	968,870
Average years employed	7	7
Annual compensation*	65,752	48,763
Standard deviation	26,794	16,618
Median compensation	63,650	48,110

National average: $64,034 with a standard deviation of $26,369 (see Chapter 4, Table 4-3).

Total respondents: 403

* includes base salary, housing or parsonage allowance, retirement contribution, life and health insurance payments, and educational funds.

Table 6-9: Annual Compensation Of Associate Pastor By Education

Highest Degree	High School	Associate	Bachelor	Master	Doctorate
Number Of Respondents	26	8	114	183	35
Salary (99%*)	24,937	26,401	33,663	37,755	39,004
Annual % Increase (73%)	8%	5%	5%	4%	7%
Parsonage (7%)	18,957	3,500	11,975	16,758	17,400
Housing (81%)	21,856	20,305	21,332	22,250	23,397
Retirement (62%)	4,030	2,879	3,138	4,808	4,391
Life Insurance (41%)	398	98	375	452	541
Health Insurance (79%)	7,814	5,559	8,931	9,311	8,701
Vacation/weeks (95%)	3	3	3	3	4
Education Fund (44%)	1,433	0	1,138	1,328	1,680
Receive Auto Allow. (87%)	88%	88%	88%	87%	94%

* The percentage following each compensation item indicates the portion of all associate pastors who received that form of compensation. The averages in each column are for those individuals who actually received that compensation item. See Chapter 3 for a full explanation of how to read this table.

Total Compensation Comparisons

Highest Degree	High School	Associate	Bachelor	Masters	Doctorate
Average attendance	688	344	755	669	757
Average church income	1,014,762	808,494	1,321,738	1,452,502	1,654,796
Average years employed	7	6	7	8	9
Annual compensation*	48,906	44,790	61,325	69,283	68,175
Standard deviation	18,134	13,058	34,223	20,638	26,427
Median compensation	44,000	45,966	57,220	67,161	64,091

National average: $64,034 with a standard deviation of $26,369 (see Chapter 4, Table 4-3).

Total respondents: 366

* includes base salary, housing or parsonage allowance, retirement contribution, life and health insurance payments, and educational funds.

Table 6-10: Annual Compensation Of Associate Pastor By Years Employed

Years Employed	0-5	6-10	11-15	over 15
Number Of Respondents	218	89	48	44
Salary (99%*)	32,604	35,707	36,595	42,366
Annual % Increase (73%)	5%	4%	6%	4%
Parsonage (7%)	13,385	14,639	14,400	30,000
Housing (81%)	21,206	21,336	24,828	24,716
Retirement (62%)	4,109	4,196	4,446	4,452
Life Insurance (41%)	401	424	337	2705
Health Insurance (79%)	8,773	9,236	8,203	10,294
Vacation/weeks (95%)	3	4	4	4
Education Fund (44%)	1,316	1,359	1,289	1,143
Receive Auto Allow. (87%)	87%	97%	90%	75%

* The percentage following each compensation item indicates the portion of all associate pastors who received that form of compensation. The averages in each column are for those individuals who actually received that compensation item. See Chapter 3 for a full explanation of how to read this table.

Total Compensation Comparisons

Years Employed	0-5	6-10	11-15	Over 15
Average attendance	627	727	846	805
Average church income	1,263,081	1,512,830	1,606,433	1,463,035
Average years employed	3	8	13	21
Annual compensation*	60,562	65,874	69,478	72,791
Standard deviation	29,937	20,978	18,980	22,020
Median compensation	56,937	67,161	66,000	69,558

National average: $64,034 with a standard deviation of $26,369 (see Chapter 4, Table 4-3).

Total respondents: 399

* includes base salary, housing or parsonage allowance, retirement contribution, life and health insurance payments, and educational funds.

Table 6-11: Annual Compensation Of Part-Time Associate Pastors By Hours Worked

Hours Per Week	1-14	15-29	30-39	All Part-time
Number of Respondents	4	27	3	68
Salary (82%*)	2,633	11,201	17,565	12,035
Annual % Increase (50%)	11%	4%	3%	4%
Parsonage (4%)	0	20,000	0	9,467
Housing (57%)	6,750	12,303	12,333	12,931
Retirement (7%)	0	1,348	0	2,459
Life Insurance (9%)	0	168	85	500
Health Insurance (26%)	0	4,660	7,194	4,877
Vacation/weeks (57%)	3	3	4	3
Education Funds (32%)	100	659	600	623
Receive Auto Allow. (81%)	100%	93%	100%	81%

* The percentage following each compensation item indicates the portion of all part-time associate pastors who received that form of compensation. The averages in each column are for those individuals who actually received that compensation item. See Chapter 3 for a full explanation of how to read this table.

Total Compensation Comparisons

Hours Worked Per Week	1-14	15-29	30-39	All Part-time
Average attendance	184	272	262	307
Average church income	464,038	477,362	509,428	507,573
Average years employed	2	4	11	5
Average hours per week	8	20	31	20
Average compensation	5,375	19,598	32,525	19,753
Ave. hourly compensation*	12.92	18.84	20.18	18.99
Ave. hourly salary**	6.33	10.77	10.90	11.57

* includes base salary, housing or parsonage allowance, retirement contribution, life and health insurance payments, and educational funds. See discussion on "rounding errors" in Chapter 3.

Chapter 7

Christian Education Directors

Employment Profile

A majority of the Christian Education Directors participating in this study serve as ordained ministers. The vast majority are college graduates, and 41% have graduate degrees. Christian Education Directors reflected the following profile:

	Full-time	Part-time
❏ Number of Respondents	248	146
❏ Ordained	53%	13%
❏ Average Years Employed	6	4
❏ Male	54%	16%
❏ Female	46%	84%
❏ Self-employed	2%	3%
❏ Church Employee	98%	97%
❏ High School Diploma	6%	16%
❏ Associate Degree	4%	8%
❏ Bachelor Degree	49%	54%
❏ Master Degree	36%	20%
❏ Doctorate	5%	2%

Compensation Analysis

The analysis below is based upon the tables found later in this chapter. The tables present compensation data according to worship attendance, church income, combinations of size and setting, gender, education, and years employed for CE Directors who serve full-time. The final table provides data for part-time CE directors based upon the number of hours worked. In this way, the CE Director's compensation can be viewed from a variety of useful perspectives. The total compensation amount found in a separate box at the bottom of each page includes the base salary, housing or parsonage amount, life and health insurance payments, retirement contribution, and educational funds.

Key Points

✎ *CE Directors are closely aligned with youth ministers in compensation trends, although, generally, the earnings of CE Directors increase more rapidly in large congregations.* Most full-time CE Directors serve in churches with an attendance over 500, with about one-third in congregations over 1,000. Overall compensation remains below the national average until a position is secured in a larger church with an average attendance over 600-700. *See Table 7-1.*

✎ *Both church income and size correlate with compensation.* Compensation tends to increase directly with the size of the church budget. From the standpoint of compensation, CE Directors are aligned with youth ministers and church administrators, but generally have higher levels of compensation in larger churches than youth ministers. Income increases significantly once the church budget exceeds $1,000,000 per year. *See Table 7-2.*

✎ *CE Directors who work in churches with an average attendance under 500 typically have an annual compensation below the national average.* Most CE Directors work in larger suburban churches, while very few work in rural settings. Generally, compensation is higher in medium size cities, suburban and urban churches. *See Tables 7-3 and 7-4.*

✎ *Significant gender differences exists for CE Directors.* Women earn lower levels of compensation than their male counterparts. A disparity of over $15,000 - $20,000 in annual total compensation has existed the past several years. Women work in smaller churches with an average attendance significantly less than men. In addition, overall church income tends to be substantially less in those churches with female CE Directors, yet in both cases, average church income exceeds $1,000,000. Women in this study were also less likely to receive fringe benefits. The difference in overall compensation can be attributed to gender more than any other variable. *See Table 7-5.*

✎ *Educational achievement has a relationship to compensation.* Overall compensation increases steadily with education. Yet, even college graduates tend to be below the national average. Forty-one percent of the full-time Christian education directors surveyed had either a master's degree or a doctorate. Those with doctoral degrees earned on average $21,000 more than the typical CE Director with a bachelor's degree. *See Table 7-6.*

✎ *Employment longevity had a slight impact on overall compensation.* Compensation increases somewhat with years of service, but with some exceptions. Those CE Directors with the highest levels of compensation tend to work in congregations with the largest incomes, regardless of years of service. Those with five or less years of service were below the national average. *See Table 7-7.*

✎ *Many CE Directors work part-time.* Hourly compensation varies with the number of hours worked. Those who work more hours take more of their compensation as fringe benefits. The typical part-time CE Director worked 22 hours per week, and had been in the church for about four years. Fairly high turnover exists. *See Table 7-8.*

Benefit Analysis

Full-time staff members. Full-time Christian education directors receive benefit packages comparable to those of other professional and ministerial staff members within the church. Yet, since fewer are ordained, a smaller percentage receive parsonage and housing allowances compared to ministerial staff members. In general, the Christian education director's average benefits are slightly less than those of associate pastors.

Part-time staff members. About 84% of part-time Christian education directors are female. Ninety-seven percent of part-time directors are church employees. Many part-time Christian education directors serve congregations with an attendance between 250-500. Part-time Christian education directors receive few benefits with the most common being an auto allowance and a two week paid vacation.

Benefits	Full-time	Part-time
❒ Housing allowance	54%	8%
❒ Parsonage provided	4%	2%
❒ Retirement	52%	9%
❒ Life insurance	37%	5%
❒ Health insurance	70%	10%
❒ Paid vacation	90%	45%
❒ Auto allowance	89%	59%
❒ Continuing education funds	43%	24%

Ten Year Compensation Trend: National Averages for Christian Education Directors

❒ 1996	$38,855
❒ 1997	$40,863
❒ 1998	$41,428
❒ 1999	$45,620
❒ 2000	$47,331
❒ 2001	$48,440
❒ 2002	$49,351
❒ 2003	$50,313
❒ 2004	$51,295
❒ 2005	$51,983

Table 7-1: Annual Compensation of CE Director by Worship Attendance

Church Attendance	0-99	100-299	300-499	500-749	750-999	over 1000
Number Of Respondents	3	30	49	59	30	72
Salary (99%*)	29,049	27,003	30,358	30,604	31,447	35,897
Annual % Increase (73%*)	3%	4%	5%	4%	4%	5%
Parsonage (4%)	0	6,000	30,000	14,728	10,086	25,700
Housing (54%)	5,000	17,856	24,927	20,069	22,027	23,442
Retirement (52%)	520	3,933	2,869	4,041	3,212	2,919
Life Insurance (37%)	375	160	301	458	274	280
Health Insurance (70%)	720	5,671	6,448	7,431	9,513	7,910
Vacation/weeks (90%)	4	3	3	3	3	3
Education Fund (43%)	720	809	1,136	1,083	1,185	1,330
Auto Allowance (89%)	67%	80%	90%	90%	100%	88%

* The percentage following each compensation item indicates the portion of CE Directors who received that form of compensation. The averages in each column are for those individuals who actually received that compensation item. See Chapter 3 for a full explanation of how to read this table.

Total Compensation Comparisons

Church Attendance	0-99	100-299	300-499	500-749	750-999	Over 1,000
Average attendance	76	191	383	600	840	1,631
Average church income	165,108	511,334	968,140	1,316,864	1,714,109	3,128,366
Average years employed	7	5	6	6	6	6
Average compensation*	31,254	37,036	46,697	51,613	51,364	63,085
Standard deviation	2,206	13,285	16,469	14,723	12,610	20,514
Median compensation	29,221	32,358	44,911	48,800	49,302	56,493

National average for all CE Directors: $51,983 with a standard deviation of $18,468 (see Chapter 4, Table 4-3).

Total respondents: 243

* includes base salary, housing or parsonage allowance, retirement contribution, life and health insurance payments, and educational funds.

Table 7-2: Annual Compensation of CE Director by Church Budget

Church Budget in $	0-249,999	250,000-499,999	500,000-749,000	750,000-999,999	1,000,000 +
Number Of Respondents	5	20	30	31	149
Salary (99%*)	26,546	27,955	28,769	27,988	33,861
Annual % Increase (73%)	4%	4%	4%	4%	4%
Parsonage (4%)	6,000	0	2,590	12,000	22,634
Housing (54%)	12,997	18,067	20,791	21,310	22,855
Retirement (52%)	2,589	3,855	3,228	2,305	3,372
Life Insurance (37%)	73	150	182	372	341
Health Insurance (70%)	1,722	4,394	7,012	5,632	7,871
Vacation/weeks (90%)	3	2	3	3	3
Education Fund (43%)	485	569	1,158	1,225	1,198
Auto Allowance (89%)	80%	70%	87%	87%	92%

* The percentage following each compensation item indicates the portion of CE Directors who received that form of compensation. The averages in each column are for those individuals who actually received that compensation item. See Chapter 3 for a full explanation of how to read this table.

Total Compensation Comparisons

Church Budget	0-249,999	250,000-499,999	500,000-749,999	750,000-999,999	1,000,000+
Average attendance	312	221	390	474	1,082
Average church income	143,065	377,774	638,193	874,457	2,347,295
Average years employed	5	4	6	7	6
Average compensation*	37,477	33,812	45,834	45,533	56,860
Standard deviation	10,181	10,291	14,828	15,275	18,230
Median compensation	30,940	31,500	43,565	45,700	53,300

National average for all CE Directors: $51,983 with a standard deviation of $18,468 (see Chapter 4, Table 4-3).

Total respondents: 235

* includes base salary, housing or parsonage allowance, retirement contribution, life and health insurance payments, and educational funds.

Table 7-3: Annual Compensation of CE Director by Church Setting and Size

Attendance Under 500	Urban	Suburban	Medium City	Small Town	Rural
Number Of Respondents	11	29'	22	17	0
Salary (99%*)	35,330	28,363	27,699	27,830	
Annual % Increase (73%)	3%	4%	4%	6%	
Parsonage (4%)	0	0	30,000	6,000	
Housing (54%)	22,784	24,158	23,822	17,984	
Retirement (52%)	2,902	3,416	3,259	2,626	
Life Insurance (37%)	255	170	315	385	
Health Insurance (70%)	6,694	5,740	6,229	6,009	
Vacation/weeks (90%)	3	3	3	3	
Education Fund (43%)	983	1,023	947	929	
Auto Allowance (89%)	100%	93%	77%	82%	

* The percentage following each compensation item indicates the portion of CE Directors who received that form of compensation. The averages in each column are for those individuals who actually received that compensation item. See Chapter 3 for a full explanation of how to read this table.

Total Compensation Comparisons

Church Size: Under 500	Urban	Suburban	Medium City	Small Town	Rural
Average attendance	327	300	295	295	
Average church income	906,165	743,671	765,866	720,042	
Average years employed	7	6	4	3	
Average compensation*	48,659	46,426	38,020	39,398	
Standard deviation	9,438	17,903	17,329	11,580	
Median compensation	46,225	41,412	30,651	35,008	

National average for all CE Directors: $51,983 with a standard deviation of $18,468 (see Chapter 4, Table 4-3).

Total respondents: 79

* includes base salary, housing or parsonage allowance, retirement contribution, life and health insurance payments, and educational funds.

Table 7-4: Annual Compensation of CE Director by Church Setting and Size

Attendance Over 499	Urban	Suburban	Medium City	Small Town	Rural
Number Of Respondents	22	65	48	18	5
Salary (99%*)	35,514	34,723	31,020	31,095	31,374
Annual % Increase (73%)	4%	4%	4%	5%	6%
Parsonage (4%)	18,320	25,700	12,000	10,086	2,590
Housing (54%)	24,315	23,492	21,356	20,243	10,110
Retirement (52%)	4,547	3,552	2,791	3,328	728
Life Insurance (37%)	358	269	299	766	104
Health Insurance (70%)	7,985	8,148	7,600	7,731	11,482
Vacation/weeks (90%)	3	3	3	3	3
Education Fund (43%)	1,282	875	1,519	1,250	925
Auto Allowance (89%)	91%	92%	96%	78%	80%

* The percentage following each compensation item indicates the portion of CE Directors who received that form of compensation. The averages in each column are for those individuals who actually received that compensation item. See Chapter 3 for a full explanation of how to read this table.

Total Compensation Comparisons

Attendance Over 499	Urban	Suburban	Medium City	Small Town	Rural
Average attendance	1,247	1,178	1,084	828	931
Average church income	3,012,006	2,499,597	1,841,249	1,577,370	1,353,823
Average years employed	6	6	7	6	4
Average compensation*	59,321	58,795	54,579	55,038	43,584
Standard deviation	18,977	17,476	14,750	21,458	15,495
Median compensation	53,910	55,600	52,386	49,286	31,172

National average for all CE Directors: $51,983 with a standard deviation of $18,468 (see Chapter 4, Table 4-3).

Total respondents: 158

* includes base salary, housing or parsonage allowance, retirement contribution, life and health insurance payments, and educational funds.

Table 7-5: Annual Compensation of CE Director by Gender

Gender	Male	Female
Number Of Respondents	132	113
Salary (99%*)	32,076	32,086
Annual % Increase (73%)	4%	4%
Parsonage (4%)	20,531	6,338
Housing (54%)	21,895	23,853
Retirement (52%)	3,399	3,129
Life Insurance (37%)	296	359
Health Insurance (70%)	8,320	5,932
Vacation/weeks (90%)	3	3
Education Fund (43%)	1,342	940
Auto Allowance (89%)	91%	88%

* The percentage following each compensation item indicates the portion of CE Directors who received that form of compensation. The averages in each column are for those individuals who actually received that compensation item. See Chapter 3 for a full explanation of how to read this table.

Total Compensation Comparisons

Gender	Male	Female
Average attendance	1,011	618
Average church income	2,014,510	1,374,728
Average years employed	6	6
Average compensation*	61,239	41,664
Standard deviation	17,926	12,947
Median compensation	59,456	41,007

National average for all CE Directors: $51,983 with a standard deviation of $18,468 (see Chapter 4, Table 4-3).

Total respondents: 245

* includes base salary, housing or parsonage allowance, retirement contribution, life and health insurance payments, and educational funds.

Table 7-6: Annual Compensation of CE Director by Education

Highest Degree	High School	Associate	Bachelor	Master	Doctorate
Number Of Respondents	14	9	104	79	11
Salary (99%*)	27,379	26,769	31,127	35,097	34,148
Annual % Increase (73%)	4%	6%	4%	4%	4%
Parsonage (4%)	0	0	17,260	18,320	0
Housing (54%)	15,150	19,523	21,775	23,513	26,718
Retirement (52%)	3,738	1,415	2,388	4,258	3,719
Life Insurance (37%)	132	67	388	359	143
Health Insurance (70%)	5,723	7,687	7,105	7,734	8,519
Vacation/weeks (90%)	3	3	3	3	3
Education Fund (43%)	833	655	921	1,287	1,840
Auto Allowance (89%)	100%	67%	89%	92%	100%

* The percentage following each compensation item indicates the portion of CE Directors who received that form of compensation. The averages in each column are for those individuals who actually received that compensation item. See Chapter 3 for a full explanation of how to read this table.

Total Compensation Comparisons

Highest Degree	High School	Associate	Bachelor	Master	Doctorate
Average attendance	651	1,068	796	872	1,209
Average church income	925,207	2,161,730	1,670,361	1,903,359	2,497,655
Average years employed	6	6	6	7	7
Average compensation*	36,956	48,039	47,443	61,440	68,689
Standard deviation	14,021	11,240	16,623	17,737	17,379
Median compensation	37,152	45,657	43,884	59,300	62,750

National average for all CE Directors: $51,983 with a standard deviation of $18,468 (see Chapter 4, Table 4-3).

Total respondents: 217

* includes base salary, housing or parsonage allowance, retirement contribution, life and health insurance payments, and educational funds.

Table 7-7: Annual Compensation of CE Director by Years Employed

Years Employed	0-5	6-10	11-15	over 15
Number Of Respondents	147	52	24	20
Salary (99%*)	30,621	34,416	32,734	35,501
Annual % Increase (73%)	4%	4%	3%	4%
Parsonage (4%)	19,374	0	1,400	0
Housing (54%)	22,061	21,942	23,214	22,236
Retirement (52%)	3,344	3,103	3,019	3,968
Life Insurance (37%)	277	269	320	614
Health Insurance (70%)	7,055	7,180	7,538	9,372
Vacation/weeks (90%)	3	3	4	4
Education Fund (43%)	1,134	1,240	865	1,135
Auto Allowance (89%)	92%	87%	75%	100%

* The percentage following each compensation item indicates the portion of CE Directors who received that form of compensation. The averages in each column are for those individuals who actually received that compensation item. See Chapter 3 for a full explanation of how to read this table.

Total Compensation Comparisons

Years Employed	0-5	6-10	11-15	Over 15
Average attendance	764	958	862	1,010
Average church income	1,561,908	2,007,316	1,875,656	1,977,570
Average years employed	3	8	13	20
Average compensation*	49,910	54,491	53,816	61,021
Standard deviation	18,472	18,878	16,402	18,773
Median compensation	47,488	52,386	50,845	56,741

National average for all CE Directors: $51,983 with a standard deviation of $18,468 (see Chapter 4, Table 4-3).

Total respondents: 243

* includes base salary, housing or parsonage allowance, retirement contribution, life and health insurance payments, and educational funds.

Table 7-8: Annual Compensation of Part-Time CE Directors by Hours Worked

Hours-per-week	1-14	15-29	30-39	All Part-time
Number Of Respondents	9	51	15	146
Salary (93%*)	6,582	12,918	24,171	14,673
Annual % Increase (60%)	3%	4%	3%	5%
Parsonage (2%)	0	12,000	3,100	7,033
Housing (8%)	0	16,739	0	10,990
Retirement (9%)	0	1,114	1,180	1,385
Life Insurance (5%)	0	0	232	207
Health Insurance (10%)	0	5,140	7,384	6,488
Vacation/weeks (45%)	3	2	2	2
Education Funds (24%)	300	758	900	740
Auto Allowance (59%)	56%	69%	80%	59%

* The percentage following each compensation item indicates the portion of part-time CE Directors who received that form of compensation. The averages in each column are for those individuals who actually received that compensation item. See Chapter 3 for a full explanation of how to read this table.

Total Compensation Comparisons

Hours Worked Per Week	1-14	15-29	30 -39	All Part-time
Average attendance	233	367	516	378
Average church income	442,578	639,983	1,057,574	711,671
Average years employed	5	4	4	4
Average hours per week	10	21	31	22
Average compensation	6,658	14,994	27,497	16,358
Ave. hourly compensation*	12.80	13.73	17.06	14.30
Average hourly salary**	12.66	11.83	14.99	12.83

Total respondents: 146

* includes base salary, housing or parsonage allowance, retirement contribution, life and health insurance payments, and educational funds (note: auto allowance is included in base salary).

Chapter 8

Youth Ministers

Employment Profile

On average, youth ministers are employed for a shorter period than other staff members. Few congregations under 100 in attendance have a youth minister. However, a church is more likely to have a youth minister than an associate pastor, Christian Education Director, choir director, business administrator, bookkeeper, or custodian. After pastors, only church secretaries serve on church staffs more frequently than youth ministers. The typical youth minister is ordained, has a college degree, and is a male. The youth ministers surveyed provided the following statistical profile:

	Full-time	Part-time
❐ Number of Respondents	407	88
❐ Ordained	67%	22%
❐ Average Years Employed	4	3
❐ Male	93%	73%
❐ Female	7%	27%
❐ Self-employed	2%	8%
❐ Church Employee	98%	92%
❐ High School Diploma	4%	26%
❐ Associate Degree	4%	7%
❐ Bachelor Degree	63%	54%
❐ Master Degree	29%	13%
❐ Doctorate	0%	0%

Compensation Analysis

The analysis below is based upon the tables found later in this chapter. The tables present compensation data according to worship attendance, church income, combinations of size and setting, gender, education, and years employed for youth pastors who serve full-time. The final table provides data for part-time youth pastors based upon the number of hours worked. In this way, the youth pastor's compensation can be viewed from a variety of useful perspectives. The total compensation amount found in a separate box at the bottom of each page includes the base salary, housing or parsonage amount, life and health insurance payments, retirement contribution, and educational funds.

Key Points

✎ ***Church attendance directly impacts the compensation of youth ministers.*** Those serving in congregations with an attendance less than 500 are below the national average; those in congregations above 500 are generally equal to or above the national average. Over one-half of youth ministers serve in the larger churches. *See Table 8-1.*

✎ ***Church income impacts total compensation.*** Neither church income nor church size, however, is decisive. Compensation levels increase more slowly for youth pastors than for other professional staff positions. The turnover rate for youth ministers is high, regardless of church size or budget. *See Table 8-2.*

✎ ***Urban and suburban churches provide the best compensation for smaller congregations.*** In most years, these congregations provide more compensation than do churches in the other geographical categories with an attendance under 500, although it varies somewhat from one year to the next. Yet all youth pastors in churches with an average attendance below 500 were below the national compensation average. *See Table 8-3.*

✎ ***Geographical setting had an impact on compensation levels within larger congregations, although it varies from year to year.*** Youth pastors in larger churches typically earn more than the national average. This is often true regardless of geographical setting. Those in suburban churches earned the most this year, but that varies from one year to the next. *See Table 8-4.*

✎ ***On average, women receive similar salaries to men, although their total compensation is significantly lower.*** Female youth pastors earn much less than their male counterparts. Male youth ministers significantly outnumber female youth ministers. Both groups tend to serve in larger congregations with higher levels of income, but females are paid less than their male counterparts. The disparity in overall earnings is based on gender. *See Table 8-5.*

✎ ***Educational achievement has a direct impact upon compensation levels of youth ministers, especially for those with a graduate degree.*** Over 90% of the youth ministers had a bachelor's degree or higher. Yet, average compensation for those with a bachelor's degree was still below the national average. Having a graduate degree resulted in significant increases in compensation. *See Table 8-6.*

✎ ***Over 90% of youth pastors serve for less than ten years with 73% serving less than five years.*** No clear variables exist that differentiate those who serve long periods from those who do not, although tenure tends to increase slightly as church income increases. *See Table 8-7.*

✎ ***In general, part-time youth ministers receive among the lowest compensation of part-time professional staff members.*** Most serve in congregations with an attendance around 250 people. *See Table 8-8.*

Benefits Analysis

Full-time staff members. Full-time youth ministers receive benefits similar to other professional staff members. In general, youth ministers are more likely to receive a housing allowance than those involved in education, music, or church administration.

Part-time staff members. Approximately 11% of the youth ministers in this sample worked part-time. Of this group, 27% were female compared to 7% for full-time youth ministers. Part-time workers often serve in smaller churches. Proportionately, salary for part-time workers was lower compared to those working full-time. Part-time workers also receive only a small fraction of the benefits of full-time staff.

Benefits	Full-time	Part-time
Housing allowance	70%	14%
Parsonage provided	6%	1%
Retirement	54%	5%
Life insurance	37%	5%
Health insurance	78%	10%
Paid vacation	94%	47%
Auto allowance	88%	52%
Continuing education funds	39%	15%

Ten Year Compensation Trend: National Averages for Youth Ministers

1996	$35,398
1997	$36,968
1998	$37,918
1999	$39,691
2000	$42,561
2001	$43,288
2002	$45,043
2003	$47,058
2004	$47,302
2005	$50,371

Table 8-1: Annual Compensation of Youth Minister by Worship Attendance

Church Attendance	0-99	100-299	300-499	500-749	750-999	over 1000
Number Of Respondents	0	76	107	82	48	87
Salary (99%*)		25,855	27,285	28,251	30,787	31,099
Annual % Increase (71%*)		7%	4%	5%	4%	5%
Parsonage (6%)		7,592	15,050	11,850	4,700	20,728
Housing (70%)		14,980	18,057	18,948	20,899	21,158
Retirement (54%)		2,295	2,902	3,049	3,180	3,155
Life Insurance (37%)		236	340	239	244	231
Health Insurance (78%)		6,779	7,631	7,511	8,582	7,895
Vacation/weeks (94%)		2	3	3	3	3
Education Fund (39%)		1,076	1,280	1,177	1,209	1,412
Auto Allowance (88%)		83%	87%	90%	92%	89%

* The percentage following each compensation item indicates the portion of youth ministers who received that form of compensation. The averages in each column are for those individuals who actually received that compensation item. See Chapter 3 for a full explanation of how to read this table.

Total Compensation Comparisons

Church Attendance	0-99	100-299	300-499	500-749	750-999	Over 1,000
Average attendance		197	386	588	839	1,594
Average church income		462,089	782,957	1,308,769	1,633,189	3,042,686
Average years employed		3	4	4	5	5
Average compensation*		42,308	48,740	49,692	54,218	58,470
Standard deviation		13,058	14,055	13,388	15,124	15,633
Median compensation		41,348	47,200	47,772	53,996	57,494

National Average: $50,371 with a standard deviation of $15,112 (see Chapter 4, Table 4-3).

Total respondents: 400

* includes base salary, housing or parsonage allowance, retirement contribution, life and health insurance payments, and educational funds.

Table 8-2: Annual Compensation of Youth Minister by Church Budget

Church Budget in $	0-249,999	250,000-499,999	500,000-749,000	750,000-999,999	1,000,000 +
Number Of Respondents	16	47	78	45	194
Salary (99%*)	26,152	26,107	25,487	27,754	30,085
Annual % Increase (71%)	5%	6%	5%	6%	4%
Parsonage (6%)	15,000	5,833	11,109	17,933	17,155
Housing (70%)	16,032	14,317	17,932	17,551	20,470
Retirement (54%)	2,436	2,536	2,618	2,126	3,307
Life Insurance (37%)	59	716	302	218	232
Health Insurance (78%)	8,599	6,810	8,144	7,026	7,758
Vacation/weeks (94%)	3	2	3	3	3
Education Fund (39%)	988	1,018	1,311	1,275	1,279
Auto Allowance (88%)	88%	83%	78%	91%	91%

* The percentage following each compensation item indicates the portion of youth ministers who received that form of compensation. The averages in each column are for those individuals who actually received that compensation item. See Chapter 3 for a full explanation of how to read this table.

Total Compensation Comparisons

Church Budget	0-249,999	250,000-499,999	500,000-749,999	750,000-999,999	1,000,000+
Average attendance	383	235	399	456	1,023
Average church income	153,569	380,048	627,802	876,421	2,243,249
Average years employed	3	3	4	4	5
Average compensation*	45,587	41,265	47,399	48,293	54,361
Standard deviation	15,627	12,903	14,175	13,896	14,946
Median compensation	43,304	40,423	46,131	46,136	53,520

National Average: $50,371 with a standard deviation of $15,112 (see Chapter 4, Table 4-3).

Total respondents: 380

* includes base salary, housing or parsonage allowance, retirement contribution, life and health insurance payments, and educational funds.

Table 8-3: Annual Compensation of Youth Minister by Church Setting and Size

Attendance Under 500	Urban	Suburban	Medium City	Small Town	Rural
Number Of Respondents	14	63	45	51	8
Salary (99%*)	26,459	27,562	26,500	26,576	22,934
Annual % Increase (71%)	8%	6%	7%	4%	4%
Parsonage (6%)	0	15,381	11,767	3,900	7,733
Housing (70%)	22,355	19,014	15,432	15,556	9,497
Retirement (54%)	2,658	2,733	2,887	2,483	2,387
Life Insurance (37%)	120	282	249	580	182
Health Insurance (78%)	4,548	7,491	8,073	7,016	7,981
Vacation/weeks (94%)	2	3	3	3	2
Education Fund (39%)	900	1,236	1,191	1,567	650
Auto Allowance (88%)	93%	87%	82%	84%	75%

* The percentage following each compensation item indicates the portion of youth ministers who received that form of compensation. The averages in each column are for those individuals who actually received that compensation item. See Chapter 3 for a full explanation of how to read this table.

Total Compensation Comparisons

Church Size: Under 500	Urban	Suburban	Medium City	Small Town	Rural
Average attendance	306	319	305	309	197
Average church income	814,434	640,262	668,727	616,057	414,402
Average years employed	2	4	3	4	5
Average compensation*	41,762	48,935	45,365	44,753	40,909
Standard deviation	17,630	14,385	15,930	10,228	9,681
Median compensation	41,252	46,586	45,720	42,000	37,824

National Average: $50,371 with a standard deviation of $15,112 (see Chapter 4, Table 4-3).

Total respondents: 181

* includes base salary, housing or parsonage allowance, retirement contribution, life and health insurance payments, and educational funds.

Table 8-4: Annual Compensation of Youth Minister by Church Setting and Size

Attendance Over 499	Urban	Suburban	Medium City	Small Town	Rural
Number Of Respondents	25	88	71	23	5
Salary (99%*)	35,601	31,015	27,044	28,464	28,076
Annual % Increase (71%)	4%	4%	5%	5%	9%
Parsonage (6%)	0	22,433	9,520	10,700	0
Housing (70%)	22,458	21,213	20,404	15,172	18,072
Retirement (54%)	3,254	3,483	2,974	2,611	1,465
Life Insurance (37%)	222	262	212	162	154
Health Insurance (78%)	6,541	8,254	8,296	7,167	7,819
Vacation/weeks (94%)	3	3	3	3	3
Education Fund (39%)	1,130	1,183	1,473	688	1,119
Auto Allowance (88%)	84%	92%	96%	74%	80%

* The percentage following each compensation item indicates the portion of youth ministers who received that form of compensation. The averages in each column are for those individuals who actually received that compensation item. See Chapter 3 for a full explanation of how to read this table.

Total Compensation Comparisons

Attendance Over 499	Urban	Suburban	Medium City	Small Town	Rural
Average attendance	1,054	1,074	1,116	758	964
Average church income	2,500,536	2,331,907	1,854,434	1,307,150	1,682,327
Average years employed	5	5	5	4	5
Average compensation*	54,517	56,954	54,341	45,767	50,918
Standard deviation	15,606	14,733	13,622	10,342	16,855
Median compensation	48,456	55,373	54,642	43,700	47,490

National Average: $50,371 with a standard deviation of $15,112 (see Chapter 4, Table 4-3).

Total respondents: 212

* includes base salary, housing or parsonage allowance, retirement contribution, life and health insurance payments, and educational funds.

Table 8-5: Annual Compensation of Youth Minister by Gender

Gender	Male	Female
Number Of Respondents	377	28
Salary (99%*)	28,428	29,731
Annual % Increase (71%)	5%	4%
Parsonage (6%)	12,983	0
Housing (70%)	18,717	19,200
Retirement (54%)	2,920	3,263
Life Insurance (37%)	264	236
Health Insurance (78%)	7,663	7,221
Vacation/weeks (94%)	3	3
Education Fund (39%)	1,239	848
Auto Allowance (88%)	88%	93%

* The percentage following each compensation item indicates the portion of youth ministers who received that form of compensation. The averages in each column are for those individuals who actually received that compensation item. See Chapter 3 for a full explanation of how to read this table.

Total Compensation Comparisons

Gender	Male	Female
Average attendance	717	560
Average church income	1,446,006	1,230,074
Average years employed	4	4
Average compensation*	50,984	42,515
Standard deviation	14,966	14,359
Median compensation	49,695	44,140

National Average: $50,371 with a standard deviation of $15,112 (see Chapter 4, Table 4-3).

Total respondents: 405

* includes base salary, housing or parsonage allowance, retirement contribution, life and health insurance payments, and educational funds.

Table 8-6: Annual Compensation of Youth Minister by Education

Highest Degree	High School	Associate	Bachelor	Master	Doctorate
Number Of Respondents	16	14	225	105	0
Salary (99%*)	24,641	22,842	28,114	29,617	
Annual % Increase (71%)	5%	6%	5%	5%	
Parsonage (6%)	36,000	29,072	11,820	8,833	
Housing (70%)	15,932	15,411	18,210	20,508	
Retirement (54%)	6,520	2,039	2,542	3,692	
Life Insurance (37%)	94	164	277	275	
Health Insurance (78%)	8,232	6,783	7,197	8,479	
Vacation/weeks (94%)	2	2	3	3	
Education Fund (39%)	1,500	1,075	1,145	1,243	
Auto Allowance (88%)	100%	93%	88%	89%	

* The percentage following each compensation item indicates the portion of youth ministers who received that form of compensation. The averages in each column are for those individuals who actually received that compensation item. See Chapter 3 for a full explanation of how to read this table.

Total Compensation Comparisons

Highest Degree	High School	Associate	Bachelor	Master	Doctorate
Average attendance	512	655	681	838	
Average church income	739,080	1,138,661	1,341,107	1,824,798	
Average years employed	4	2	4	5	
Average compensation*	44,805	43,321	47,819	57,062	
Standard deviation	15,282	19,381	13,757	13,171	
Median compensation	40,124	41,338	46,586	55,240	

National Average: $50,371 with a standard deviation of $15,112 (see Chapter 4, Table 4-3).

Total respondents: 360

* includes base salary, housing or parsonage allowance, retirement contribution, life and health insurance payments, and educational funds.

Table 8-7: Annual Compensation of Youth Minister by Years Employed

Years Employed	0-5	6-10	11-15	over 15
Number Of Respondents	295	76	25	6
Salary (99%*)	27,912	29,978	30,586	31,800
Annual % Increase (71%)	5%	4%	3%	3%
Parsonage (6%)	13,684	9,475	0	0
Housing (70%)	18,073	20,220	20,289	21,625
Retirement (54%)	2,781	3,509	2,733	3,368
Life Insurance (37%)	249	329	173	176
Health Insurance (78%)	7,054	9,102	8,748	7,617
Vacation/weeks (94%)	3	3	4	4
Education Fund (39%)	1,154	1,512	942	700
Auto Allowance (88%)	88%	87%	88%	100%

* The percentage following each compensation item indicates the portion of youth ministers who received that form of compensation. The averages in each column are for those individuals who actually received that compensation item. See Chapter 3 for a full explanation of how to read this table.

Total Compensation Comparisons

Years Employed	0-5	6-10	11-15	Over 15
Average attendance	623	947	831	1,139
Average church income	1,325,473	1,759,671	1,562,272	1,841,860
Average years employed	2	8	13	20
Average compensation*	48,108	57,365	54,454	54,510
Standard deviation	14,811	14,020	11,221	13,621
Median compensation	46,586	55,240	53,918	52,316

National Average: $50,371 with a standard deviation of $15,112 (see Chapter 4, Table 4-3).

Total respondents: 402

* includes base salary, housing or parsonage allowance, retirement contribution, life and health insurance payments, and educational funds.

Table 8-8: Annual Compensation of Part-Time Youth Ministers by Hours Worked

Hours-per-week	1-14	15-29	30-39	All Part-time
Number Of Respondents	13	20	6	88
Salary (93%*)	7,565	12,771	14,639	12,181
Annual % Increase (44%)	4%	4%	4%	6%
Parsonage (1%)	0	0	0	6,200
Housing (14%)	15,600	12,600	17,414	13,348
Retirement (5%)	0	497	1,437	1,658
Life Insurance (5%)	0	945	56	356
Health Insurance (10%)	6,329	1,195	1,756	5,534
Vacation/weeks (47%)	2	2	2	2
Education Funds (15%)	0	440	1,700	581
Auto Allowance (52%)	46%	70%	83%	52%

* The percentage following each compensation item indicates the portion of part-time youth ministers who received that form of compensation. The averages in each column are for those individuals who actually received that compensation item. See Chapter 3 for a full explanation of how to read this table.

Total Compensation Comparisons

Hours Worked Per Week	1-14	15-29	30-39	All Part-time
Average attendance	173	353	369	255
Average church income	289,832	667,487	563,409	493,489
Average years employed	2	2	3	3
Average hours per week	8	19	30	17
Average compensation	8,670	14,324	18,828	14,145
Ave. hourly compensation*	20.84	14.50	12.07	16.00
Average hourly salary**	18.19	12.93	9.38	13.78

Total respondents: 88

* includes base salary, housing or parsonage allowance, retirement contribution, life and health insurance payments, and educational funds. See discussion of "rounding errors" in Chapter 3.

Chapter 9

Choir and Music Directors

Employment Profile

A significant percentage of music and choir directors serve on a part-time basis. While men occupy most of the full-time positions, part-time positions divide about equally between males and females. Choir and music directors provided the following employment profile:

	Full-time	Part-time
❐ Number of Respondents	277	253
❐ Ordained	61%	10%
❐ Average years employed	7	7
❐ Male	87%	52%
❐ Female	13%	48%
❐ Self-employed	1%	6%
❐ Church Employee	99%	94%
❐ High School Diploma	8%	15%
❐ Associate's Degree 18%	4%	
❐ Bachelor's Degree	46%	47%
❐ Master's Degree	41%	26%
❐ Doctorate	4%	8%

Compensation Analysis

The analysis below is based upon the tables found later in this chapter. The tables present compensation data according to worship attendance, church income, combinations of size and setting, gender, education, and years employed for music and choir directors who serve full-time. The final table provides data for part-time music and choir directors based upon the number of hours worked. In this way, the compensation of music and choir directors can be viewed from a variety of useful perspectives. The total compensation amount found in a separate box at the bottom of each page includes the base salary, housing or parsonage amount, life and health insurance payments, retirement contribution, and educational funds.

Key Points

✎ *Compensation increases steadily with church size.* While music and choir directors start out low, they experience one of the fastest rate of increases of all staff positions. The greatest gains occur when the attendance reaches 200, and then increases sreadily after that. *See Table 9-1.*

✎ *Church income impacts compensation in a pattern similar to church attendance.* Again, compensation starts off low, but increases rapidly. The vast majority of choir directors work in churches with an annual income over $1,000,000. These individuals receive, on average, $10,000 to $20,000 a year more compensation than choir directors in churches with an annual income under $500,000. *See Table 9-2.*

✎ *Over the past several years, compensation has fluctuated by geographical setting in smaller congregations.* This year the highest level of compensation was found in churches located in urban areas. In previous years, suburban and medium size city locations provided the highest compensation for smaller congregations under 500 in attendance. Churches with an attendance under 500 provided a compensation package below the national average. *See Table 9-3.*

✎ *Larger churches, except those in small towns or rural settings, tend to be above or near the national average.* Urban, suburban, and churches in medium size cities provide the highest levels of compensation, with urban churches providing higher salaries. The majority of churches in this category were above the national average. *See Table 9-4.*

✎ *Male directors earned considerably more than did female directors.* On average, females earn substantially less compensation than their male counterparts. Women actually had a higher salary, but fewer females received fringe benefits. Also, few women had full-time positions, and those that did tended to work in congregations with lower budgets. Gender, however, is the key variable affecting compensation. *See Table 9-5.*

✎ *College graduates receive substantially higher compensation than do high school graduates; having a graduate degree tended to increase the compensation above the national average.* College graduates earned over $7,000 more than those with a high school education. This year, as in previous years, significant increases occurred for those having a master's or a doctoral degree. As a group, they tend to be the only ones above the national average. *See Table 9-6.*

✎ *Length of employment has some impact upon compensation levels.* Those with less than five years of service received a compensation below the national average. This represented 56% of all music and choir directors. Compensation rose slowly, and somewhat inconsistently, with years of service. *See Table 9-7.*

✎ *Most part-time directors work about 16 hours or less per week.* Historically, more music and choir directors serve part-time than full-time. Generally, hourly compensation is the highest for those working the fewest hours per week. *See Table 9-8.*

Benefits

Full-time staff members. Most fringe benefits are comparable to those of other professional staff members. Few received a parsonage allowance, although 61% did receive a housing allowance.

Part-time staff members. Part-time workers receive few benefits, but they generally work only about 16 hours per week.

Benefits Part-time	Full-time	Part-time
Housing allowance	61%	6%
Parsonage provided	3%	1%
Retirement	55%	6%
Life insurance	44%	2%
Health insurance	71%	4%
Paid vacation	91%	36%
Auto allowance	86%	47%
Continuing education funds	36%	11%

Ten Year Compensation Trend: National Average for Music and Choir Directors

1996	$43,790
1997	$43,598
1998	$45,603
1999	$49,383
2000	$50,911
2001	$53,200
2002	$55,046
2003	$56,875
2004	$57,279
2005	$60,316

Table 9-1: Annual Compensation of Music of Choir Director by Worship Attendance

Church Attendance	0-99	100-299	300-499	500-749	750-999	over 1000
Number Of Respondents	0	33	59	63	36	81
Salary (99%*)		31,973	31,946	37,671	39,178	40,193
Annual % Increase (72%*)		4%	4%	3%	4%	4%
Parsonage (3%)		0	9,067	22,000	15,600	23,375
Housing (61%)		20,445	19,106	21,741	22,364	27,522
Retirement (55%)		3,317	4,421	4,376	4,539	3,696
Life Insurance (44%)		352	339	383	371	285
Health Insurance (71%)		8,463	7,921	8,024	8,746	8,464
Vacation/weeks (91%)		3	3	3	3	3
Education Fund (36%)		641	1,282	1,006	984	1,267
Auto Allowance (86%)		82%	81%	89%	92%	88%

* The percentage following each compensation item indicates the portion of music or choir directors who received that form of compensation. The averages in each column are for those individuals who actually received that compensation item. See Chapter 3 for a full explanation of how to read this table.

Total Compensation Comparisons At A Glance*

Worship Attendance	0-99	100-299	300-499	500-749	750-999	over 1000
Average attendance		211	385	596	840	1,575
Average church income		609,823	819,987	1,471,580	1,838,936	2,949,107
Average years employed		5	7	8	6	9
Average compensation*		50,048	50,451	59,481	61,035	72,620
Standard deviation		14,690	13,479	14,873	20,479	22,635
Median compensation		45,700	48,648	58,356	62,970	69,700

National average: $60,316 with a standard deviation of $20,343 (see Chapter 4, Table 4-3)

Total respondents: 272

* includes base salary, housing or parsonage allowance, retirement contribution, life and health insurance payments, and educational funds.

Table 9-2: Annual Compensation of Music or Choir Director by Church Budget

Church Budget in $	0-249,999	250,000-499,999	500,000-749,000	750,000-999,999	1,000,000 +
Number Of Respondents	8	16	35	29	170
Salary (99%*)	27,521	30,793	31,274	34,740	39,358
Annual % Increase (72%)	3%	5%	4%	4%	4%
Parsonage (3%)	0	5,100	16,000	0	22,017
Housing (61%)	26,040	13,783	18,017	21,489	25,068
Retirement (55%)	4,553	3,244	4,754	3,850	4,038
Life Insurance (44%)	55	1,137	292	342	306
Health Insurance (71%)	13,207	6,443	7,483	7,026	8,534
Vacation/weeks (91%)	3	3	3	3	3
Education Fund (36%)	0	700	1,007	1,067	1,153
Auto Allowance (86%)	75%	69%	86%	79%	89%

* The percentage following each compensation item indicates the portion of music or choir directors who received that form of compensation. The averages in each column are for those individuals who actually received that compensation item. See Chapter 3 for a full explanation of how to read this table.

Total Compensation Comparisons

Church Budget	0-249,999	250,000-499,999	500,000-749,999	750,000-999,999	1,000,000+
Average attendance	271	260	387	456	1,041
Average church income	129,328	386,493	621,446	885,680	2,303,036
Average years employed	6	4	8	7	8
Average compensation*	55,627	41,912	51,061	51,846	66,390
Standard deviation	32,978	10,255	10,857	15,582	19,417
Median compensation	44,800	42,640	48,919	47,700	64,007

National average: $60,316 with a standard deviation of $20,343 (see Chapter 4, Table 4-3)

Total respondents: 258

* includes base salary, housing or parsonage allowance, retirement contribution, life and health insurance payments, and educational funds.

Table 9-3: Annual Compensation of Music or Choir Director by Church Setting and Size

Attendance Under 500	Urban	Suburban	Medium City	Small Town	Rural
Number Of Respondents	8	29	25	27	0
Salary (99%*)	36,956	28,851	33,480	31,596	
Annual % Increase (72%)	3%	4%	4%	4%	
Parsonage (3%)	0	9,600	17,000	600	
Housing (61%)	24,950	22,287	19,718	14,314	
Retirement (55%)	3,662	3,168	5,061	4,441	
Life Insurance (44%)	98	195	179	602	
Health Insurance (71%)	10,228	6,909	10,848	7,404	
Vacation/weeks (91%)	3	3	3	3	
Education Fund (36%)	800	867	954	1,575	
Auto Allowance (86%)	88%	83%	84%	74%	

* The percentage following each compensation item indicates the portion of music or choir directors who received that form of compensation. The averages in each column are for those individuals who actually received that compensation item. See Chapter 3 for a full explanation of how to read this table.

Total Compensation Comparisons

Attendance Under 500	Urban	Suburban	Medium City	Small Town	Rural
Average attendance	287	332	317	323	
Average church income	863,850	730,798	770,388	667,897	
Average years employed	4	6	7	8	
Average compensation*	54,254	49,225	50,090	47,963	
Standard deviation	19,036	14,269	15,976	14,439	
Median compensation	42,160	46,331	46,061	47,200	

National average: $60,316 with a standard deviation of $20,343 (see Chapter 4, Table 4-3)

Total respondents: 89

* includes base salary, housing or parsonage allowance, retirement contribution, life and health insurance payments, and educational funds.

Table 9-4: Annual Compensation of Music or Choir Director by Church Setting and Size

Attendance Over 499	Urban	Suburban	Medium City	Small Town	Rural
Number Of Respondents	28	74	54	16	4
Salary (99%*)	43,153	41,299	35,260	36,990	35,231
Annual % Increase (72%)	3%	4%	4%	4%	6%
Parsonage (3%)	0	24,500	0	15,600	0
Housing (61%)	26,986	28,567	23,559	15,543	13,920
Retirement (55%)	4,436	4,442	3,645	3.914	940
Life Insurance (44%)	360	348	247	422	146
Health Insurance (71%)	7,200	9,013	8,658	7,001	6,920
Vacation/weeks (91%)	3	3	3	3	3
Education Fund (36%)	1,150	951	1,272	938	888
Auto Allowance (86%)	86%	88%	94%	88%	75%

* The percentage following each compensation item indicates the portion of music or choir directors who received that form of compensation. The averages in each column are for those individuals who actually received that compensation item. See Chapter 3 for a full explanation of how to read this table.

Total Compensation Comparisons

Attendance Over 499	Urban	Suburban	Medium City	Small Town	Rural
Average attendance	972	1,132	1,145	900	1,069
Average church income	2,426,343	2,431,709	1,943,221	1,642,030	1,891,248
Average years employed	8	9	8	4	5
Average compensation*	65,840	70,356	64,051	55,324	50,118
Standard deviation	19,308	23,991	13,537	16,635	17,502
Median compensation	62,970	69,386	64,751	52,345	41,300

National average: $60,316 with a standard deviation of $20,343 (see Chapter 4, Table 4-3)

Total respondents: 176

* includes base salary, housing or parsonage allowance, retirement contribution, life and health insurance payments, and educational funds.

Table 9-5: Annual Compensation of Music or Choir Director by Gender

Gender	Male	Female
Number Of Respondents	239	35
Salary (99%*)	36,236	40,956
Annual % Increase (72%)	4%	4%
Parsonage (3%)	17,589	0
Housing (61%)	23,359	16,500
Retirement (55%)	4,060	4,064
Life Insurance (44%)	306	539
Health Insurance (71%)	8,337	7,541
Vacation/weeks (91%)	3	3
Education Fund (36%)	1,136	814
Auto Allowance (86%)	89%	71%

* The percentage following each compensation item indicates the portion of music or choir directors who received that form of compensation. The averages in each column are for those individuals who actually received that compensation item. See Chapter 3 for a full explanation of how to read this table.

Total Compensation Comparisons

Gender	Male	Female
Averahe attendance	854	598
Average church income	1,790,917	1,278,789
Average years employed	7	8
Average compensation*	62,070	48,334
Standard deviation	20,002	17,698
Median compensation	58,870	45,352

National average: $60,316 with a standard deviation of $20,343 (see Chapter 4, Table 4-3)

Total respondents: 274

* includes base salary, housing or parsonage allowance, retirement contribution, life and health insurance payments, and educational funds.

Table 9-6: Annual Compensation of Music or Choir Director by Education

Highest Degree	High School	Associate	Bachelor	Master	Doctorate
Number Of Respondents	20	4	112	102	10
Salary (99%*)	27,224	21,042	34,892	38,708	52,908
Annual % Increase (72%)	5%	4%	4%	4%	4%
Parsonage (3%)	0	0	12,186	17,000	0
Housing (61%)	23,543	19,000	22,904	23,321	31,000
Retirement (55%)	3,534	0	3,568	4,476	5,362
Life Insurance (44%)	153	148	374	327	242
Health Insurance (71%)	7,936	11,956	7,968	8,511	7,763
Vacation/weeks (91%)	3	4	3	3	4
Education Fund (36%)	850	600	949	1,221	986
Auto Allowance (86%)	85%	67%	84%	89%	100%

* The percentage following each compensation item indicates the portion of music or choir directors who received that form of compensation. The averages in each column are for those individuals who actually received that compensation item. See Chapter 3 for a full explanation of how to read this table.

Total Compensation Comparisons

Highest Degree	High School	Associate	Bachelor	Master	Doctorate
Average attendance	704	704	868	783	1,016
Average church income	1,250,244	1,977,704	1,742,725	1,713,782	2,805,711
Average years employed	5	3	7	8	10
Average compensation*	50,442	55,511	57,712	63,643	78,062
Standard deviation	15,258	18,947	20,349	18,158	16,757
Median compensation	47,700	45,750	54,100	62,250	70,207

National average: $60,316 with a standard deviation of $20,343 (see Chapter 4, Table 4-3)

Total respondents: 248

* includes base salary, housing or parsonage allowance, retirement contribution, life and health insurance payments, and educational funds.

Table 9-7: Annual Compensation of Music or Choir Director by Years Employed

Years Employed	0-5	6-10	11-15	over 15
Number Of Respondents	151	49	36	34
Salary (99%*)	34,966	38,342	39,918	40,807
Annual % Increase (72%)	4%	4%	4%	3%
Parsonage (3%)	20,171	0	1,500	0
Housing (61%)	22,140	23,353	22,120	27,618
Retirement (55%)	3,767	3,538	4,570	4,907
Life Insurance (44%)	297	381	312	416
Health Insurance (71%)	8,011	10,653	7,412	7,486
Vacation/weeks (91%)	3	3	4	4
Education Fund (36%)	1,207	1,192	793	836
Auto Allowance (86%)	89%	86%	83%	82%

* The percentage following each compensation item indicates the portion of music or choir directors who received that form of compensation. The averages in each column are for those individuals who actually received that compensation item. See Chapter 3 for a full explanation of how to read this table.

Total Compensation Comparisons

Years Employed	0-5	6-10	11-15	over 15
Average attendance	786	845	769	924
Average church income	1,649,538	1,745,743	1,700,717	2,068,964
Average years employed	3	8	13	22
Average compensation*	56,682	61,801	62,809	71,261
Standard deviation	19,880	20,594	18,968	20,687
Median compensation	54,800	60,128	58,631	71,566

National average: $60,316 with a standard deviation of $20,343 (see Chapter 4, Table 4-3)

Total respondents: 270

* includes base salary, housing or parsonage allowance, retirement contribution, life and health insurance payments, and educational funds.

Table 9-8: Annual Compensation of Part-Time Music/Choir Directors by Hours Worked

Hours-per-week	1-14	15-29	30-39	All Part-time
Number Of Respondents	50	61	10	253
Salary (92%*)	10,619	14,810	26,821	12,846
Annual % Increase (55%)	4%	4%	8%	4%
Parsonage (1%)	0	6,000	2,700	7,113
Housing (6%)	3,616	13,042	0	13,442
Retirement (6%)	867	1,601	685	2,021
Life Insurance (2%)	0	96	168	435
Health Insurance (4%)	0	2,404	3,448	3,505
Vacation/weeks (36%)	3	2	3	2
Education Funds (11%)	500	842	500	724
Auto Allowance (47%)	46%	64%	90%	47%

* The percentage following each compensation item indicates the portion of part-timemusic or choir directors who received that form of compensation. The averages in each column are for those individuals who actually received that compensation item. See Chapter 3 for a full explanation of how to read this table.

Total Compensation Comparisons

Hours Worked Per Week	1-14	15-29	30-39	All Part-time
Average attendance	246	378	783	281
Average church income	476,614	703,092	1,064,202,	540,272
Average years employed	7	5	6	7
Average hours per week	9	19	31	16
Average compensation	10,802	16,324	28,261	13,844
Ave. hourly compensation**	23.08	16.52	17.53	16.64
Average hourly salary*	22.69	14.99	16.64	15.44

Total respondents: 253

* includes base salary, housing or parsonage allowance, retirement contribution, life and health insurance payments, and educational funds. See discussion on "rounding errors" in Chapter 3.

Chapter 10

Church Administrators

Employment Profile

Church administrators tend to serve in larger churches. In this study, 28% of those working full-time were ordained ministers, although this percentage declines significantly for those serving part-time. Men hold a majority of the full-time positions while women are in a majority for those working part-time. This group of administrators provided the following employment profile:

	Full-time	Part-time
❏ Number of Respondents	314	83
❏ Ordained	28%	7%
❏ Average years employed	7	6
❏ Male	56%	40%
❏ Female	44%	60%
❏ Self-employed	0%	8%
❏ Church Employee	100%	92%
❏ High School Diploma	13%	19%
❏ Associate's Degree	12%	13%
❏ Bachelor's Degree	45%	38%
❏ Master's Degree	26%	24%
❏ Doctorate	4%	6%

Compensation Analysis

The analysis below is based upon the tables found later in this chapter. The tables present compensation data according to worship attendance, church income, combinations of size and setting, gender, education, and years employed for administrators who serve full-time. The final table provides data for part-time administrators based upon the number of hours worked. In this way, the administrator's compensation can be viewed from a variety of useful perspectives. The total compensation amount found in a separate box at the bottom of each page includes the base salary, housing or parsonage amount, life and health insurance payments, retirement contribution, and educational funds.

Key Points

✎ *Compensation increases with church size.* Base salary and total compensation increases with church size. Business administrators most often worked in larger churches. Nearly 60% worked in churches with an attendance over 500. About 26% worked in churches over 1,000. The national average compensation corresponded to a church attendance of about 600. *See Table 10-1.*

✎ *Church budget has a direct impact on compensation.* Generally, compensation increases as church income increases. Over half of the administrators participating in this study worked in churches with income over $1,000,000. *See Table 10-2.*

✎ *Urban, suburban and churches located in medium size cities provide the highest compensation for smaller congregations.* Few rural churches employ business administrators. On average, business administrators in congregations with an attendance under 500 tend to receive compensation levels below the national average regardless of the church's geographical setting. *See Table 10-3.*

✎ *Urban and suburban churches tend to provid the highest compensation for larger churches (attendance above 500).* About 40% of administrators in this group work in suburban churches. Those serving in rural settings and small towns earn considerably less than their urban and suburban counterparts. *See Table 10-4.*

✎ *On average, male church business administrators received over $25,000 more compensation than did females.* This represented the largest earning gap of any church staff position. In terms of salary alone, women earned about $10,000 per year less. Women earn below the national average even though they serve in churches with incomes and attendances that should reflect higher compensation levels. *See Table 10-5.*

✎ *College graduates receive substantially higher compensation than do high school graduates; having a graduate degree increases the compensation.* College graduates earned over $15,000 more than those with only a high school education. Significant increases occurred over the national average once the administrator earned a graduate degree. *See Table 10-6.*

✎ *Length of employment had no significant impact upon compensation levels.* Those serving on average 22 years earned less than those servng eight years. Fifty-four percent of church business administrators had worked for their church an average of three years. *See Table 10-7.*

✎ *Most part-time administrators work about 26 hours per week.* On average, they earn significantly less per hour than a full-time administrator. This is due to the decreased levels of compensation provided to the increased number of female part-time administrators. *See Table 10-8.*

Benefits

Full-time staff members. Most fringe benefits were slightly less than those of other professional staff members. Fewer church business administrators received housing or parsonage allowances reflecting the mixed ministerial status of this group.

Part-time staff members. Eighteen percent of the church business administrators surveyed worked part-time. Females comprised over half of this group.

Benefits Part-time	Full-time	Part-time
☐ Housing allowance	28%	5%
☐ Parsonage provided	2%	0%
☐ Retirement	47%	16%
☐ Life insurance	34%	5%
☐ Health insurance	65%	16%
☐ Paid vacation	91%	52%
☐ Auto allowance	85%	63%
☐ Continuing education funds	33%	12%

Ten Year Compensation Trend:
National Averages for Church Administrators

☐	1996	$36,871
☐	1997	$37,413
☐	1998	$40,207
☐	1999	$42,277
☐	2000	$44,768
☐	2001	$48,064
☐	2002	$47,305
☐	2003	$50,615
☐	2004	$49,907
☐	2005	$53,153

Table 10-1: Annual Compensation of Administrator by Worship Attendance

Church Attendance	0-99	100-299	300-499	500-749	750-999	over 1000
Number Of Respondents	3	59	66	59	40	81
Salary (99%*)	18,733	30,288	33,107	41,294	44,050	48,570
Annual % Increase (73%*)	2%	6%	5%	5%	5%	5%
Parsonage (2%)	0	20,000	14,175	0	4,700	10,360
Housing (28%)	0	16,271	20,276	24,232	21,837	26,340
Retirement (47%)	0	2,073	3,014	3,618	3,689	3,148
Life Insurance (34%)	0	417	260	626	624	304
Health Insurance (65%)	5,620	6,585	6,205	6,933	8,645	7,632
Vacation/weeks (91%)	4	3	3	3	3	3
Education Fund (33%)	0	655	959	1,126	1,170	1,209
Auto Allowance (85%)	67%	71%	85%	88%	90%	89%

* The percentage following each compensation item indicates the portion of administrators who received that form of compensation. The averages in each column are for those individuals who actually received that compensation item. See Chapter 3 for a full explanation of how to read this table.

Total Compensation Comparisons At A Glance*

Worship Attendance	0-99	100-299	300-499	500-749	750-999	over 1000
Average attendance	73	206	383	607	836	1,710
Average church income	210,593	529,276	906,437	1,484,770	1,636,308	3,171,073
Average years employed	7	8	8	5	6	7
Average compensation*	20,607	35,268	42,688	55,896	59,243	70,662
Standard deviation	9,636	14,380	15,729	17,449	21,480	20,878
Median compensation	23,000	33,268	40,008	53,500	53,939	69,712

National average: $53,153 with a standard deviation of $22,489 (see Chapter 4, Table 4-3)

Total respondents: 308

* includes base salary, housing or parsonage allowance, retirement contribution, life and health insurance payments, and educational funds.

Table 10-2: Annual Compensation of Administrator by Church Budget

Church Budget in $	0-249,999	250,000-499,999	500,000-749,000	750,000-999,999	1,000,000 +
Number Of Respondents	13	26	45	34	173
Salary (99%*)	29,957	30,788	31,438	30,842	45,788
Annual % Increase (73%)	4%	3%	8%	4%	5%
Parsonage (2%)	0	0	20,000	14,175	8,473
Housing (28%)	29,700	7,200	18,194	18,300	24,767
Retirement (47%)	3,330	2,428	1,924	2,214	3,588
Life Insurance (34%)	161	224	369	274	470
Health Insurance (65%)	11,962	5,732	5,819	5,452	7,503
Vacation/weeks (91%)	3	3	3	3	3
Education Fund (33%)	1,000	812	859	1,208	1,122
Auto Allowance (85%)	62%	73%	76%	79%	90%

* The percentage following each compensation item indicates the portion of administrators who received that form of compensation. The averages in each column are for those individuals who actually received that compensation item. See Chapter 3 for a full explanation of how to read this table.

Total Compensation Comparisons

Church Budget	0-249,999	250,000-499,999	500,000-749,999	750,000-999,999	1,000,000+
Average attendance	194	230	368	435	1,084
Average church income	187,399	381,865	600,010	859,926	2,339,963
Average years employed	6	8	7	7	7
Average compensation*	41,186	34,711	38,657	37,998	63,841
Standard deviation	32,144	10,597	13,087	12,292	19,704
Median compensation	26,500	33,404	36,365	36,645	60,624

National average: $53,153 with a standard deviation of $22,489 (see Chapter 4, Table 4-3)

Total respondents: 291

* includes base salary, housing or parsonage allowance, retirement contribution, life and health insurance payments, and educational funds.

Table 10-3: Annual Compensation of Administrator by Church Setting and Size

Attendance Under 500	Urban	Suburban	Medium City	Small Town	Rural
Number Of Respondents	22	39	24	32	6
Salary (99%*)	34,957	33,688	31,141	28,258	27,579
Annual % Increase (73%)	6%	7%	4%	4%	3%
Parsonage (2%)	0	20,000	0	14,175	0
Housing (28%)	31,667	18,916	17,378	15,967	7,200
Retirement (47%)	3,147	1,914	3,747	1,463	4,259
Life Insurance (34%)	394	285	240	203	304
Health Insurance (65%)	6,706	6,333	5,193	6,265	8,448
Vacation/weeks (91%)	3	3	3	3	3
Education Fund (33%)	893	893	534	900	0
Auto Allowance (85%)	86%	85%	75%	72%	67%

* The percentage following each compensation item indicates the portion of administrators who received that form of compensation. The averages in each column are for those individuals who actually received that compensation item. See Chapter 3 for a full explanation of how to read this table.

Total Compensation Comparisons

Attendance Under 500	Urban	Suburban	Medium City	Small Town	Rural
Average attendance	294	300	302	297	238
Average church income	894,536	617,933	765,992	727,154	442,240
Average years employed	9	7	9	8	6
Average compensation*	44,416	41,176	37,860	33,430	35,172
Standard deviation	18,470	14,971	12,476	14,128	12,441
Median compensation	43,249	40,057	36,645	30,936	34,440

National average: $53,153 with a standard deviation of $22,489 (see Chapter 4, Table 4-3)

Total respondents: 123

* includes base salary, housing or parsonage allowance, retirement contribution, life and health insurance payments, and educational funds.

Table 10-4: Annual Compensation of Administrator by Church Setting and Size

Attendance Over 499	Urban	Suburban	Medium City	Small Town	Rural
Number Of Respondents	26	75	59	13	3
Salary (99%*)	47,738	47,846	41,194	39,921	48,167
Annual % Increase (73%)	4%	5%	5%	5%	0%
Parsonage (2%)	0	2,000	11,710	0	0
Housing (28%)	25,688	28,127	22,212	24,350	0
Retirement (47%)	4,558	3,413	2,855	3,454	1,500
Life Insurance (34%)	483	473	277	1,088	166
Health Insurance (65%)	8,937	7,401	7,871	6,804	3,723
Vacation/weeks (91%)	3	3	3	3	3
Education Fund (33%)	1,200	970	1,380	1,000	1,138
Auto Allowance (85%)	88%	87%	95%	77%	100%

* The percentage following each compensation item indicates the portion of administrators who received that form of compensation. The averages in each column are for those individuals who actually received that compensation item. See Chapter 3 for a full explanation of how to read this table.

Total Compensation Comparisons

Attendance Over 499	Urban	Suburban	Medium City	Small Town	Rural
Average attendance	1,016	1,229	1,202	833	1,166
Average church income	2,544,112	2,476,342	2,022,843	1,704,253	1,811,520
Average years employed	8	6	5	6	3
Average compensation*	68,065	65,971	60,468	54,814	53,204
Standard deviation	19,277	21,900	17,876	19,838	22,262
Median compensation	65,393	62,594	58,363	48,930	30,795

National average: $53,153 with a standard deviation of $22,489 (see Chapter 4, Table 4-3)

Total respondents: 176

* includes base salary, housing or parsonage allowance, retirement contribution, life and health insurance payments, and educational funds.

Table 10-5: Annual Compensation of Administrator by Gender

Gender	Male	Female
Number Of Respondents	174	137
Salary (99%*)	44,181	34,062
Annual % Increase (73%)	5%	6%
Parsonage (2%)	9,899	20,000
Housing (28%)	24,320	16,478
Retirement (47%)	3,362	2,713
Life Insurance (34%)	346	535
Health Insurance (65%)	7,898	5,512
Vacation/weeks (91%)	3	3
Education Fund (33%)	1,136	892
Auto Allowance (85%)	89%	81%

* The percentage following each compensation item indicates the portion of administrators who received that form of compensation. The averages in each column are for those individuals who actually received that compensation item. See Chapter 3 for a full explanation of how to read this table.

Total Compensation Comparisons

Gender	Male	Female
Averahe attendance	1,014	520
Average church income	2,024,052	1,084,521
Average years employed	6	8
Average compensation*	64,402	38,833
Standard deviation	20,113	15,793
Median compensation	61,564	36,220

National average: $53,153 with a standard deviation of $22,489 (see Chapter 4, Table 4-3)

Total respondents: 311

* includes base salary, housing or parsonage allowance, retirement contribution, life and health insurance payments, and educational funds.

Table 10-6: Annual Compensation of Administrator by Education

Highest Degree	High School	Associate	Bachelor	Master	Doctorate
Number Of Respondents	35	33	127	72	10
Salary (99%*)	30,578	33,244	40,788	48,444	39,056
Annual % Increase (73%)	4%	5%	6%	5%	5%
Parsonage (2%)	0	20,000	8,473	14,175	0
Housing (28%)	24,550	24,775	23,997	24,491	22,120
Retirement (47%)	2,469	1,847	3,321	3,648	4,652
Life Insurance (34%)	690	198	411	402	557
Health Insurance (65%)	6,150	5,473	6,897	7,980	8,474
Vacation/weeks (91%)	3	3	3	3	3
Education Fund (33%)	857	535	1,048	1,186	1,425
Auto Allowance (85%)	89%	76%	83%	93%	90%

* The percentage following each compensation item indicates the portion of administrators who received that form of compensation. The averages in each column are for those individuals who actually received that compensation item. See Chapter 3 for a full explanation of how to read this table.

Total Compensation Comparisons

Highest Degree	High School	Associate	Bachelor	Master	Doctorate
Average attendance	451	644	836	1,043	970
Average church income	837,404	1,417,977	1,687,089	2,065,095	2,584,100
Average years employed	8	9	6	7	9
Average compensation*	38,038	40,778	54,126	68,093	58,757
Standard deviation	15,614	16,133	22,790	19,213	22,364
Median compensation	33,268	39,100	48,930	67,272	59,302

National average: $53,153 with a standard deviation of $22,489 (see Chapter 4, Table 4-3)

Total respondents: 277

* includes base salary, housing or parsonage allowance, retirement contribution, life and health insurance payments, and educational funds.

Table 10-7: Annual Compensation of Administrator by Years Employed

Years Employed	0-5	6-10	11-15	over 15
Number Of Respondents	167	81	28	31
Salary (99%*)	39,007	41,371	39,008	40,110
Annual % Increase (73%)	6%	4%	6%	4%
Parsonage (2%)	10,360	20,000	4,700	14,175
Housing (28%)	21,703	24,404	26,125	25,716
Retirement (47%)	2,834	3,421	4,037	3,273
Life Insurance (34%)	432	347	480	572
Health Insurance (65%)	7,040	7,726	7,258	5,681
Vacation/weeks (91%)	3	3	4	4
Education Fund (33%)	,148	1,109	713	696
Auto Allowance (85%)	86%	85%	89%	77%

* The percentage following each compensation item indicates the portion of administrators who received that form of compensation. The averages in each column are for those individuals who actually received that compensation item. See Chapter 3 for a full explanation of how to read this table.

Total Compensation Comparisons

Years Employed	0-5	6-10	11-15	over 15
Average attendance	746	956	827	533
Average church income	1,504,047	1,827,550	1,937,049	1,462,614
Average years employed	3	8	13	22
Average compensation*	50,467	55,727	61,353	52,594
Standard deviation	21,167	23,531	22,925	24,324
Median compensation	46,848	52,400	62,013	43,161

National average: $53,153 with a standard deviation of $22,489 (see Chapter 4, Table 4-3)

Total respondents: 307

* includes base salary, housing or parsonage allowance, retirement contribution, life and health insurance payments, and educational funds.

Table 10-8: Annual Compensation of Part-Time Administrators by Hours Worked

Hours-per-week	1-14	15-29	30-39	All Part-time
Number Of Respondents	0	19	24	83
Salary (94%*)		18,151	26,771	19,400
Annual % Increase (55%)		4%	3%	5%
Parsonage (0%)		0	0	0
Housing (5%)		0	24,000	22,353
Retirement (16%)		936	2,572	2,062
Life Insurance (5%)		0	846	572
Health Insurance 16(%)		3,278	3,559	4,848
Vacation/weeks (52%)		2	3	3
Education Funds (12%)		600	900	740
Auto Allowance (63%)		89%	75%	63%

* The percentage following each compensation item indicates the portion of part-timeadministrators who received that form of compensation. The averages in each column are for those individuals who actually received that compensation item. See Chapter 3 for a full explanation of how to read this table.

Total Compensation Comparisons

Hours Worked Per Week	1-14	15-29	30-39	All Part-time
Average attendance		407	440	376
Average church income		647,561	878,333	685,040
Average years employed		5	6	6
Average hours per week		20	32	26
Average compensation		18,628	32,159	21,822
Ave. hourly compensation**		17.91	19.33	16.14
Average hourly salary*		17.45	16.09	14.35

Total respondents: 83

* includes base salary, housing or parsonage allowance, retirement contribution, life and health insurance payments, and educational funds. See discussion on "rounding errors" in Chapter 3.

Chapter 11

Church Bookkeepers

Employment Profile

From an employment standpoint, church bookkeepers are aligned with church secretaries and custodians. Very few are ordained ministers. They tend to be hourly paid church employees with the overwhelming number female, whether full-time or part-time. An increasing number are college graduates. The church bookkeepers surveyed provided the following employment profile:

	Full-time	Part-time
❑ Number of Respondents	197	228
❑ Ordained	1%	1%
❑ Average years employed	9	7
❑ Male	8%	13%
❑ Female	92%	87%
❑ Self-employed	0%	7%
❑ Church Employee	100%	93%
❑ High School Diploma	31%	28%
❑ Associate Degree	16%	15%
❑ Bachelor Degree	47%	51%
❑ Master Degree	5%	4%
❑ Doctorate	1%	2%

Compensation Analysis

The analysis below is based upon the tables found later in this chapter. The tables present compensation data according to worship attendance, church income, combinations of size and setting, gender, education, and years employed for bookkeepers who serve full-time. The final table provides data for part-time bookkeepers based upon the number of hours worked. In this way, the bookkeeper's compensation can be viewed from a variety of useful perspectives. The total compensation amount found in a separate box at the bottom of each page includes the base salary, housing or parsonage amount, life and health insurance payments, retirement contribution, and educational funds.

Key Points

✎ *The compensation of bookkeepers increases significantly with church size.* Total compensation increases with attendance, with the fastest growth occurring once church attendance exceeds 1,000. About one-third of all church bookkeepers work in churches of that size or larger. *See Table 11-1.*

✎ *Compensation increases slowly with increases in church income.* About 65% of bookkeepers work in congregations with an annual income in excess of $1,000,000. The national average compensation was not achieved until the church's income, on average, was over $1,500,000. *See Table 11-2.*

✎ *Urban churches provided the highest compensation for bookkeepers in smaller churches (attendance under 500).* Most curches with an average attendance under 500 provided compensation below the national average. *See Table 11-3.*

✎ *Urban and suburban churches provided the highest compensation for bookkeepers in larger churches (attendance over 500).* In churches with an average attendance over 500, those in small towns and rural settings were below the national average. *See Table 11-4.*

✎ *Female bookkeepers earned less than did males.* Historically, females have earned less than their male counterparts, although three years ago they earned slightly more. Men represent only a small percentage of all bookkeepers. This year, females earned about $2,700 less in total compensation. The average compensation for men was above the national average. Both men and women tend to work in larger congregations. *See Table 11-5.*

✎ *Educational achievement has a minor impact on total compensation.* Bookkeepers with college degrees earned slightly more than the national average, while those without a college education tended to earn slightly less. This year those with a master's degree earned significantly more than the national average, although two years ago they earned less than the national average. *See Table 11-6.*

✎ *Generally, length of employment has only a minor impact upon the compensation of church bookkeepers.* About 45% of full-time bookkeepers had worked an average of three years at their church. These individuals earned earned about the same as the group with an average of 8 years of service. While overall compensation was up for those with longer tenures, that is not always the case. *See Table 11-7.*

✎ *Most part-time bookkeepers work about 18 hours per week.* Historically, their average hourly compensation is higher than that of secretaries and custodians, but less than the other staff positions examined in this study. *See Table 11-8.*

Benefit Analysis

Full-time staff members. Church bookkeepers receive less benefits than do administrators or ministerial staff. The percentage of those who receive health insurance, retirement contributions, or educational funds is notably less. Only 1% received a housing allowance. Bookkeepers, however, do receive better benefits than secretaries and were about the same as custodians.

Part-time staff members. Over half of the bookkeepers surveyed worked part-time for their churches. The majority worked about 18 hours per week. Eighty-seven percent of part-time bookkeepers were women. Part-time bookkeepers earned less than other part-time professional staff, and slightly more than did part-time secretaries or custodians. As with other part-time positions, few received fringe benefits other than a vacation or an auto allowance.

Benefits	Full-time	Part-time
❏ Housing allowance	1%	0%
❏ Parsonage provided	0%	0%
❏ Retirement	44%	7%
❏ Life insurance	36%	6%
❏ Health insurance	56%	6%
❏ Paid vacation	95%	33%
❏ Auto allowance	81%	56%
❏ Continuing education funds	17%	5%

Ten Year Compensation Trend: National Averages for Bookkeepers

❏ 1996	$23,548
❏ 1997	$23,839
❏ 1998	$24,623
❏ 1999	$26,229
❏ 2000	$27,992
❏ 2001	$29,220
❏ 2002	$29,398
❏ 2003	$30,457
❏ 2004	$32,765
❏ 2005	$33,336

Table 11-1: Annual Compensation of Bookkeeper by Worship Attendance

Church Attendance	0-99	100-299	300-499	500-749	750-999	over 1000
Number Of Respondents	0	24	41	38	27	62
Salary (99%*)		28,429	25,099	28,552	30,468	33,736
Annual % Increase (77%*)		3%	4%	4%	5%	5%
Parsonage (0%)		0	0	0	0	0
Housing (1%)		0	14,400	0	0	0
Retirement (44%)		1,818	1,508	2,058	1,968	1,949
Life Insurance (36%)		145	169	325	406	271
Health Insurance (56%)		5,813	4,969	4,447	5,689	4,652
Vacation/weeks (95%)		3	3	3	3	3
Education Fund (17%)		425	310	907	433	902
Auto Allowance (81%)		75%	71%	76%	93%	89%

* The percentage following each compensation item indicates the portion of bookkeepers who received that form of compensation. The averages in each column are for those individuals who actually received that compensation item. See Chapter 3 for a full explanation of how to read this table.

Total Compensation Comparisons

Worship Attendance	0-99	100-299	300-499	500-749	750-999	over 1,000
Average attendance		227	388	595	842	1,725
Average church income		598,953	931,095	1,587,254	1,826,823	3,395,581
Average years employed		11	9	7	8	9
Average compensation*		30,995	28,779	32,560	34,472	37,586
Standard deviation		12,228	8,947	8,912	10,646	12,427
Median compensation		28,500	27,243	31,600	32,700	36,500

National average: $33,336 with a standard deviation of $11,181 (see Chapter 4, Table 4-3)

Total respondents: 192

* includes base salary, housing or parsonage allowance, retirement contribution, life and health insurance payments, and educational funds.

Table 11-2: Annual Compensation of Bookkeeper by Church Budget

Church Budget in $	0-249,999	250,000-499,999	500,000-749,000	750,000-999,999	1,000,000 +
Number Of Respondents	6	7	31	21	122
Salary (99%*)	25,493	20,426	23,634	26,524	32,175
Annual % Increase (77%)	4%	4%	4%	4%	4%
Parsonage (0%)	0	0	0	0	0
Housing (1%)	0	0	14,400	0	0
Retirement (44%)	721	2,100	1,458	1,533	2,083
Life Insurance (36%)	24	0	182	134	315
Health Insurance (56%)	5,988	5,080	5,945	3,961	4,865
Vacation/weeks (95%)	2	2	3	3	3
Education Fund (17%)	250	200	480	300	704
Auto Allowance (81%)	83%	57%	68%	76%	86%

* The percentage following each compensation item indicates the portion of bookkeepers who received that form of compensation. The averages in each column are for those individuals who actually received that compensation item. See Chapter 3 for a full explanation of how to read this table.

Total Compensation Comparisons

Church Budget	0-249,999	250,000-499,999	500,000-749,999	750,000-999,999	1,000,000+
Average attendance	230	210	389	419	1,146
Average church income	169,617	401,870	620,459	855,541	2,611,290
Average years employed	9	4	8	10	9
Average compensation*	27,655	23,531	27,814	28,950	36,185
Standard deviation	11,070	8,638	9,835	7,788	11,272
Median compensation	25,400	19,050	25,000	28,300	34,878

National average: $33,336 with a standard deviation of $11,181 (see Chapter 4, Table 4-3)

Total respondents: 187

* includes base salary, housing or parsonage allowance, retirement contribution, life and health insurance payments, and educational funds.

Table 11-3: Annual Compensation of Bookkeeper by Church Setting and Size

Attendance Under 500	Urban	Suburban	Medium City	Small Town	Rural
Number Of Respondents	10	16	19	18	0
Salary (99%*)	31,429	29,079	26,146	19,482	
Annual % Increase (77%)	4%	3%	4%	4%	
Parsonage (0%)	0	0	0	0	
Housing (1%)	0	0	0	14,400	
Retirement (44%)	2,879	1,360	1,466	1,304	
Life Insurance (36%)	0	141	178	20	
Health Insurance (56%)	4,495	5,527	3,868	6,349	
Vacation/weeks (95%)	3	3	3	3	
Education Fund (17%)	475	0	213	250	
Auto Allowance (81%)	90%	81%	58%	61%	

* The percentage following each compensation item indicates the portion of bookkeepers who received that form of compensation. The averages in each column are for those individuals who actually received that compensation item. See Chapter 3 for a full explanation of how to read this table.

Total Compensation Comparisons

Attendance Under 500	Urban	Suburban	Medium City	Small Town	Rural
Average attendance	284	342	300	330	
Average church income	846,806	803,472	796,240	648,631	
Average years employed	11	10	11	8	
Average compensation*	34,186	32,854	28,708	22,848	
Standard deviation	13,782	8,967	7,217	7,221	
Median compensation	34,963	30,000	28,300	22,050	

National average: $33,336 with a standard deviation of $11,181 (see Chapter 4, Table 4-3)

Total respondents: 63

* includes base salary, housing or parsonage allowance, retirement contribution, life and health insurance payments, and educational funds.

Table 11-4: Annual Compensation of Bookkeeper by Church Setting and Size

Attendance Over 499	Urban	Suburban	Medium City	Small Town	Rural
Number Of Respondents	18	52	42	10	0
Salary (99%*)	32,617	33,067	29,881	26,733	
Annual % Increase (77%)	5%	5%	5%	5%	
Parsonage (0%)	0	0	0	0	
Housing (1%)	0	0	0	0	
Retirement (44%)	2,795	2,048	1,681	1,454	
Life Insurance (36%)	555	274	177	542	
Health Insurance (56%)	4,883	4,625	5,168	4,956	
Vacation/weeks (95%)	3	3	3	2	
Education Fund (17%)	800	645	789	200	
Auto Allowance (81%)	78%	85%	95%	70%	

* The percentage following each compensation item indicates the portion of bookkeepers who received that form of compensation. The averages in each column are for those individuals who actually received that compensation item. See Chapter 3 for a full explanation of how to read this table.

Total Compensation Comparisons

Attendance Over 499	Urban	Suburban	Medium City	Small Town	Rural
Average attendance	977	1,322	1,219	906	
Average church income	2,704,016	2,795,785	2,202,414	1,724,748	
Average years employed	7	8	8	9	
Average compensation*	37,067	37,136	34,200	31,055	
Standard deviation	8,479	10,662	12,021	11,352	
Median compensation	37,140	36,210	32,339	29,900	

National average: $33,336 with a standard deviation of $11,181 (see Chapter 4, Table 4-3)

Total respondents: 122

* includes base salary, housing or parsonage allowance, retirement contribution, life and health insurance payments, and educational funds.

Table 11-5: Annual Compensation of bookkeeper by Gender

Gender	Male	Female
Number Of Respondents	15	181
Salary (99%*)	32,698	29,323
Annual % Increase (77%)	5%	4%
Parsonage (0%)	0	0
Housing (1%)	0	14,400
Retirement (44%)	1,617	1,929
Life Insurance (36%)	621	250
Health Insurance (56%)	4,040	4,986
Vacation/weeks (95%)	3	3
Education Fund (17%)	1,325	628
Auto Allowance (81%)	93%	80%

* The percentage following each compensation item indicates the portion of bookkeepers who received that form of compensation. The averages in each column are for those individuals who actually received that compensation item. See Chapter 3 for a full explanation of how to read this table.

Total Compensation Comparisons

Gender	Male	Female
Average attendance	965	891
Average church income	1,746,295	1,934,010
Average years employed	9	9
Average compensation*	35,817	33,110
Standard deviation	10,206	11,286
Median compensation	29,900	32,100

National average: $33,336 with a standard deviation of $11,181 (see Chapter 4, Table 4-3)

Total respondents: 196

* includes base salary, housing or parsonage allowance, retirement contribution, life and health insurance payments, and educational funds.

Table 11-6: Annual Compensation of bookkeeper by Education

Highest Degree	High School	Associate	Bachelor	Master	Doctorate
Number Of Respondents	50	26	78	8	0
Salary (99%*)	26,936	29,073	31,725	35,763	
Annual % Increase (77%)	4%	4%	5%	5%	
Parsonage (0%)	0	0	0	0	
Housing (1%)	14,400	0	0	0	
Retirement (44%)	1,909	1,574	1,867	2,266	
Life Insurance (36%)	252	196	339	234	
Health Insurance (56%)	4,921	5,381	5,159	2,725	
Vacation/weeks (95%)	3	3	3	3	
Education Fund (17%)	697	442	686	1,500	
Auto Allowance (81%)	86%	81%	85%	88%	

* The percentage following each compensation item indicates the portion of bookkeepers who received that form of compensation. The averages in each column are for those individuals who actually received that compensation item. See Chapter 3 for a full explanation of how to read this table.

Total Compensation Comparisons

Highest Degree	High School	Associate	Bachelor	Master	Doctorate
Average attendance	857	832	966	1,449	
Average church income	1,658,584	1,477,163	2,221,855	3,332,800	
Average years employed	10	7	7	9	
Average compensation*	31,452	33,134	35,207	37,881	
Standard deviation	12,147	8,430	11,264	13,560	
Median compensation	30,172	31,307	33,600	30,000	

National average: $33,336 with a standard deviation of $11,181 (see Chapter 4, Table 4-3)

Total respondents: 162

* includes base salary, housing or parsonage allowance, retirement contribution, life and health insurance payments, and educational funds.

Table 11-7: Annual Compensation of Bookkeeper by Years Employed

Years Employed	0-5	6-10	11-15	over 15
Number Of Respondents	86	50	25	31
Salary (99%*)	29,498	28,319	27,681	34,475
Annual % Increase (77%)	5%	4%	3%	3%
Parsonage (0%)	0	0	0	0
Housing (1%)	0	0	14,400	0
Retirement (44%)	1,725	1,842	1,886	2,222
Life Insurance (36%)	297	251	339	236
Health Insurance (56%)	4,680	4,303	6,091	5,265
Vacation/weeks (95%)	2	3	4	4
Education Fund (17%)	836	638	513	483
Auto Allowance (81%)	83%	80%	80%	87%

* The percentage following each compensation item indicates the portion of bookkeepers who received that form of compensation. The averages in each column are for those individuals who actually received that compensation item. See Chapter 3 for a full explanation of how to read this table.

Total Compensation Comparisons

Years Employed	0-5	6-10	11-15	over 15
Average attendance	973	771	776	986
Average church income	1,845,345	1,707,352	1,594,886	2,614,583
Average years employed	3	8	13	23
Average compensation*	32,971	30,781	34,086	38,817
Standard deviation	11,615	9,580	11,233	10,993
Median compensation	31,629	29,153	32,100	35,200

National average: $33,336 with a standard deviation of $11,181 (see Chapter 4, Table 4-3)

Total respondents: 192

* includes base salary, housing or parsonage allowance, retirement contribution, life and health insurance payments, and educational funds.

Table 11-8: Annual Compensation of Part-Time Bookkeepers by Hours Worked

Hours-per-week	1-14	15-29	30-39	All Part-time
Number Of Respondents	41	70	19	228
Salary (94%*)	5,197	12,511	24,391	11,051
Annual % Increase (60%)	3%	4%	3%	4%
Parsonage (0%)	0	0	0	0
Housing (0%)	0	0	0	0
Retirement (7%)	551	750	1,977	1,662
Life Insurance (6%)	0	185	209	224
Health Insurance (6%)	410	0	2,781	3,094
Vacation/weeks (33%)	2	3	3	2
Education Funds (5%)	0	522	338	519
Auto Allowance (56%)	56%	66%	63%	56%

* The percentage following each compensation item indicates the portion of part-time bookkeepers who received that form of compensation. The averages in each column are for those individuals who actually received that compensation item. See Chapter 3 for a full explanation of how to read this table.

Total Compensation Comparisons

Hours Worked Per Week	1-14	15-29	30-39	All Part-time
Average attendance	318	477	773	434
Average church income	583,282	885,955	1,315,760	789,570
Average years employed	7	6	10	7
Average hours per week	8	21	30	18
Average compensation	5,223	12,611	26,627	11,511
Average hourly compensation*	12.56	11.55	17.07	12.30
Average hourly salary	12.49	11.46	15.64	11.81

Total respondents: 228

* includes base salary, housing or parsonage allowance, retirement contribution, life and health insurance payments, and educational funds. See discussion on "rounding errors" in Chapter 3.

Chapter 12

Church Secretaries

Employment Profile

The title of church secretary can encompass a number of clerical and administrative roles within the church office. Church secretaries are the second most common paid position on the church staff following pastors. Almost all are church employees with 98% being female. Less than 1% percent served as ordained ministers, although almost all viewed their work as both a ministry and a job. Most have worked as business secretaries and over 60% work in the church they attend. The secretaries surveyed provided the following employment profile:

	Full-time	Part-time
Number of Respondents	1,100	1,055
Ordained	0%	1%
Average Years Employed	8	6
Male	2%	2%
Female	98%	98%
Self-employed	0%	2%
Church Employee	100%	98%
High School Diploma	51%	51%
Associate Degree	21%	22%
Bachelor Degree	25%	24%
Master Degree	3%	3%
Doctorate	0%	0%

Compensation Analysis

The analysis below is based upon the tables found later in this chapter. The tables present compensation data according to worship attendance, church income, combinations of size and setting, gender, education, and years employed for church secretaries who serve full-time. The final table provides data for part-time church secretaries based upon the number of hours worked. In this way, the church secretary's compensation can be viewed from a variety of useful perspectives. The total compensation amount found in a separate box at the bottom of each page includes the base salary, housing or parsonage amount, life and health insurance payments, retirement contribution, and educational funds.

Key Points

✎ *Secretarial compensation is affected by church size.* Compensation for church secretaries increases gradually with size. The national average compensation corresponds with a church size of about 400 people. Secretaries serving in smaller congregations are paid substantially less than the national average. *See Table 12-1.*

✎ *Church income has an impact on compensation.* Similar to attendance, total compensation increases with church income. The national average compensation was obtained with church incomes approaching $400,000. The biggest increases occurred once church income passed $1,000,000. *See Table 12-2.*

✎ *Urban, suburban and churches in medium size cities provided the best compensation for smaller churches.* Only suburban and urban churches achieved the national average compensation. Churches in other settings paid less, although the fringe benefits were comparable. *See Table 12-3.*

✎ *Urban and suburban churches provided the best compensation for larger churches with an average attendance over 500.* All larger churches provided a compensation package near or above the national average, except for those in small towns or rural settings. *See Table 12-4.*

✎ *Over 97% of these church secretaries were women.* The few men who participated in this study reported an annual compensation higher than that of the women. Yet, the male secretaries in this study tended to serve congregations with smaller incomes. On average, the male secretaries had worked half as long as their female counterparts. *See Table 12-5.*

✎ *Educational attainment has little impact on compensation.* The true controlling factors were attendance and church income. Those secretaries with college degrees earned more than those who were high school graduates, although it is not clear that the higher income is attributable to education. *See Table 12-6.*

✎ *Years employed had some impact on compensation.* A secretary who had worked thirteen years earned more than one who had worked twenty-one years. Over half of these secretaries had worked on average only three years. About 13% had worked more than fifteen years. *See Table 12-7.*

✎ *Part-time secretaries earn less per hour than do their full-time counterparts.* The typical part-time church secretary works about three days per week. Some part-time secretaries do not receive a salary, but rather receive their compensation as fringe benefits. *See Table 12-8.*

Benefit Analysis

Full-time staff members. Church secretaries receive less benefits for full-time work than ministerial and professional staff. Housing allowances were negligible. Only 37% received health insurance, less than any other position surveyed in this study.

Part-time staff members. Forty-nine percent of church secretaries worked part-time. Most work less than 24 hours per week. Ninety-eight percent of church secretaries working part-time were employees of the church and 2% were self-employed. Few benefits were provided for part-time church secretaries apart from paid vacation.

Benefits	Full-time	Part-time
❏ Housing allowance	0%	0%
❏ Parsonage provided	0%	0%
❏ Retirement	24%	5%
❏ Life insurance	12%	1%
❏ Health insurance	37%	4%
❏ Paid vacation	87%	56%
❏ Auto allowance	26%	12%
❏ Continuing education funds	17%	8%

Ten Year Compensation Trend:
National Averages for Church Secretaries

❏ 1996	$19,178
❏ 1997	$20,232
❏ 1998	$20,353
❏ 1999	$21,354
❏ 2000	$21,965
❏ 2001	$23,316
❏ 2002	$24,132
❏ 2003	$24,875
❏ 2004	$25,007
❏ 2005	$26,624

Table 12-1: Annual Compensation of Secretary by Worship Attendance

Church Attendance	0-99	100-299	300-499	500-749	750-999	over 1,000
Number Of Respondents	56	426	252	152	66	135
Salary (95%*)	20,346	22,695	24,691	24,602	27,450	28,873
Annual % Increase (59%)	3%	4%	4%	4%	4%	4%
Parsonage (0%)	0	0	0	0	0	0
Housing (0%)	0	0	0	0	0	0
Retirement (24%)	1,638	1,753	1,652	1,935	2,156	1,600
Life Insurance (12%)	344	399	298	336	436	246
Health Insurance (37%)	5,672	4,494	4,967	5,103	5,005	5,099
Vacation/weeks (87%)	3	3	3	3	3	3
Education Funds (17%)	350	374	504	509	365	601
Auto Allowance (26%)	7%	11%	25%	38%	48%	52%

* The percentage following each compensation item indicates the portion of church secretaries who received that form of compensation. The averages in each column are for those individuals who actually received that compensation item. See Chapter 3 for a full explanation of how to read this table.

Total Compensation Comparisons

Church Attendance	0-99	100-299	300-499	500-749	750-999	over 1,000
Average attendance	67	193	366	585	840	1,812
Average church income	193,968	364,269	694,101	1,194,859	1,716,885	2,949,204
Average years employed	9	7	7	7	8	9
Average compensation*	22,040	24,495	26,800	27,829	29,994	31,667
Standard deviation	10,115	8,798	8,196	9,611	11,644	11,955
Median compensation	20,000	24,000	26,385	27.391	31,295	31,250

National average: $26,624 with a standard deviation of $9,849 (see Chapter 4, Table 4-3).

Total respondents: 1,087

* includes base salary, housing or parsonage allowance, retirement contribution, life and health insurance payments, and educational funds.

Table 12-2: Annual Compensation of Secretary by Church Income

Church Income in $	0-249,999	250,000-499,999	500,000-749,000	750,000-999,999	1,000,000 +
Number Of Respondents	137	259	148	71	264
Salary (95%*)	19,871	23,263	24,925	24,231	28,135
Annual % Increase (59%)	3%	4%	4%	4%	4%
Parsonage 0(%)	0	0	0	0	0
Housing (0%)	0	0	0	0	0
Retirement (24%)	1,543	1,723	1,790	1,587	1,924
Life Insurance (12%)	262	468	205	251	330
Health Insurance (37%)	3,836	5,134	4,445	5,135	4,977
Vacation/weeks (87%)	3	3	3	3	3
Education Funds (17%)	322	388	453	764	509
Auto Allowance (26%)	12%	10%	21%	39%	60%

* The percentage following each compensation item indicates the portion of church secretaries who received that form of compensation. The averages in each column are for those individuals who actually received that compensation item. See Chapter 3 for a full explanation of how to read this table.

Total Compensation Comparisons

Church Budget	0-249,999	250,000-499,999	500,000-749,999	750,000-999,999	1,000,000+
Average attendance	187	226	378	439	1,044
Average church income	161,222	350,717	601,129	859,285	2,158,591
Average years employed	8	8	7	7	9
Average compensation*	21,108	25,507	27,066	27,303	31,622
Standard deviation	7,699	6,872	8,580	8,258	9,703
Median compensation	20,410	25,000	27,585	28,292	31,250

National average: $26,624 with a standard deviation of $9,849 (see Chapter 4, Table 4-3).

Total respondents: 879

* includes base salary, housing or parsonage allowance, retirement contribution, life and health insurance payments, and educational funds.

Table 12-3: Annual Compensation of Secretary by Church Setting And Size

Attendance Under 500	Urban	Suburban	Medium City	Small Town	Rural
Number Of Respondents	59	208	192	218	48
Salary (95%*)	25,655	24,987	23,007	21,904	20,700
Annual % Increase (59%)	3%	4%	3%	4%	3%
Parsonage (0%)	0	0	0	0	0
Housing (0%)	0	0	0	0	0
Retirement (24%)	2,008	1,669	1,934	1,613	867
Life Insurance (12%)	945	240	307	339	78
Health Insurance (37%)	5,455	4,724	4,650	5,106	3,181
Vacation/weeks (87%)	3	3	3	3	3
Education Funds (17%)	341	259	432	365	417
Auto Allowance (26%)	25%	17%	15%	15%	10%

* The percentage following each compensation item indicates the portion of church secretaries who received that form of compensation. The averages in each column are for those individuals who actually received that compensation item. See Chapter 3 for a full explanation of how to read this table.

Total Compensation Comparisons

Attendance Under 500	Urban	Suburban	Medium City	Small Town	Rural
Average attendance	256	259	245	231	200
Average church income	568,879	509,336	460,452	428,743	284,367
Average years employed	9	6	7	8	8
Average compensation*	28,730	26,774	24,955	23,703	22,114
Standard deviation	10,678	9,454	7,809	8,711	7,351
Median compensation	28,292	26,220	24,032	22,414	21,950

National average: $26,624 with a standard deviation of $9,849 (see Chapter 4, Table 4-3).

Total respondents: 725

* includes base salary, housing or parsonage allowance, retirement contribution, life and health insurance payments, and educational funds.

Table 12-4: Annual Compensation of Secretary by Church Setting And Size

Attendance Over 499	Urban	Suburban	Medium City	Small Town	Rural
Number Of Respondents	46	141	104	47	10
Salary (95%*)	29,112	28,815	24,985	23,054	22,227
Annual % Increase (59%)	3%	4%	4%	4%	3%
Parsonage (0%)	0	0	0	0	0
Housing (0%)	0	0	0	0	0
Retirement (24%)	2,249	2,079	1,663	1,096	555
Life Insurance (12%)	532	244	337	253	166
Health Insurance (37%)	5,029	5,520	4,968	4,524	3,566
Vacation/weeks (87%)	3	3	3	3	3
Education Funds (17%)	583	386	701	315	592
Auto Allowance (26%)	50%	48%	51%	23%	20%

* The percentage following each compensation item indicates the portion of church secretaries who received that form of compensation. The averages in each column are for those individuals who actually received that compensation item. See Chapter 3 for a full explanation of how to read this table.

Total Compensation Comparisons

Attendance Over 499	Urban	Suburban	Medium City	Small Town	Rural
Average attendance	1,209	1,232	1,046	768	919
Average church income	1,994,142	2,340,969	1,752,014	1,275,529	1,300,599
Average years employed	9	8	8	7	8
Average compensation*	32,951	31,713	27,942	25,490	24,671
Standard deviation	10,040	11,511	10,692	8,554	8,170
Median compensation	34,154	31,200	28,600	24,092	22,800

National average: $26,624 with a standard deviation of $9,849 (see Chapter 4, Table 4-3).

Total respondents: 348

* includes base salary, housing or parsonage allowance, retirement contribution, life and health insurance payments, and educational funds.

Table 12-5: Annual Compensation of Secretary by Gender

Gender	Male	Female
Number Of Respondents	18	1,073
Salary (95%*)	26,782	24,354
Annual % Increase (59%)	4%	4%
Parsonage (0%)	0	0
Housing (0%)	0	0
Retirement (24%)	2,308	1,776
Life Insurance (12%)	127	328
Health Insurance (37%)	4,597	4,857
Vacation/weeks (87%)	3	3
Education Funds (17%)	600	439
Auto Allowance (26%)	39%	25%

* The percentage following each compensation item indicates the portion of church secretaries who received that form of compensation. The averages in each column are for those individuals who actually received that compensation item. See Chapter 3 for a full explanation of how to read this table.

Total Compensation Comparisons

Gender	Male	Female
Average attendance	416	524
Average church income	728,217	951,289
Average years employed	4	8
Average compensation*	30,429	26,574
Standard deviation	7,564	9,899
Median compensation	30,184	25,847

National average: $26,624 with a standard deviation of $9,849 (see Chapter 4, Table 4-3).

Total respondents: 1,091

* includes base salary, housing or parsonage allowance, retirement contribution, life and health insurance payments, and educational funds.

Table 12-6: Annual Compensation of Secretary by Education

Highest Degree	High School	Associate	Bachelor	Master	Doctorate
Number Of Respondents	483	206	237	32	0
Salary (95%*)	23,399	24,720	26,045	25,580	
Annual % Increase (59%)	4%	3%	4%	3%	
Parsonage (0%)	0	0	0	0	
Housing (0%)	0	0	0	0	
Retirement (24%)	1,624	1,574	2,144	2,428	
Life Insurance (12%)	256	393	417	262	
Health Insurance (37%)	4,740	4,800	5,019	4,265	
Vacation/weeks (87%)	3	3	3	3	
Education Funds (17%)	430	459	367	425	
Auto Allowance (26%)	24%	15%	28%	16%	

* The percentage following each compensation item indicates the portion of church secretaries who received that form of compensation. The averages in each column are for those individuals who actually received that compensation item. See Chapter 3 for a full explanation of how to read this table.

Total Compensation Comparisons

Highest Degree	High School	Associate	Bachelor	Master	Doctorate
Average attendance	493	448	574	771	
Average church income	820,507	779,824	1,195,135	698,847	
Average years employed	8	7	8	5	
Average compensation	25,577	26,750	28,483	27,919	
Standard deviation	9,541	10,365	9,642	8,251	
Median compensation	24,505	26,492	28,122	28,000	

National average: $26,624 with a standard deviation of $9,849 (see Chapter 4, Table 4-3).

Total respondents: 958

* includes base salary, housing or parsonage allowance, retirement contribution, life and health insurance payments, and educational funds.

Table 12-7: Annual Compensation of Secretary by Years Employed

Years Employed	0-5	6-10	11-15	over 15
Number Of Respondents	547	271	122	146
Salary (95%*)	23,503	25,067	25,393	25,110
Annual % Increase (59%)	4%	3%	4%	4%
Parsonage (0%)	0	0	0	0
Housing (0%)	0	0	0	0
Retirement (24%)	1,657	1,834	2,247	1,637
Life Insurance (12%)	261	354	413	285
Health Insurance (37%)	4,148	5,347	5,513	5,022
Vacation/weeks (87%)	2	3	3	4
Education Funds (17%)	505	426	408	287
Auto Allowance (26%)	21%	31%	34%	29%

* The percentage following each compensation item indicates the portion of church secretaries who received that form of compensation. The averages in each column are for those individuals who actually received that compensation item. See Chapter 3 for a full explanation of how to read this table.

Total Compensation Comparisons

Years Employed	0-5	6-10	11-15	over 15
Average attendance	496	498	653	538
Average church income	841,738	948,131	1,194,878	1,082,221
Average years employed	3	8	13	21
Average compensation*	24,903	27,945	28,609	28,343
Standard deviation	9,909	9,371	9,366	9,392
Median compensation	24,000	27,573	28,324	27,518

National average: $26,624 with a standard deviation of $9,849 (see Chapter 4, Table 4-3).

Total respondents: 1,086

* includes base salary, housing or parsonage allowance, retirement contribution, life and health insurance payments, and educational funds.

Table 12-8: Annual Compensation of Part-Time Secretaries by Hours Worked

Hours-per-week	under 15	15-29	30-39	All Part-time
Number Of Respondents	103	594	211	1,055
Salary (89%*)	5,500	11,108	16,593	11,626
Annual % Increase (41%)	5%	4%	4%	4%
Parsonage (0%)	0	0	0	0
Housing (0%)	0	0	0	0
Retirement (5%)	2,000	1,021	1,272	1,206
Life Insurance (1%)	345	214	227	261
Health Insurance (4%)	0	4,245	3,734	4,088
Vacation/weeks (56%)	3	2	2	2
Education Funds (8%)	100	255	252	250
Auto Allowance (12%)	6%	8%	16%	12%

* The percentage following each compensation item indicates the portion of part-time church secretaries who received that form of compensation. The averages in each column are for those individuals who actually received that compensation item. See Chapter 3 for a full explanation of how to read this table.

Total Compensation Comparisons

Hours Worked Per Week	under 15	15-29	30-39	All Part-time
Average attendance	113	192	255	200
Average church income	159,642	408,737	411,888	378,535
Average years employed	7	6	6	6
Average hours per week	9	21	31	22
Average compensation	5,531	11,302	16,929	11,862
Ave. hourly compensation*	11.82	10.35	10.50	10.37
Average hourly salary**	11.75	10.17	10.29	10.16

Total respondents: 1,055

* includes base salary, housing or parsonage allowance, retirement contribution, life and health insurance payments, and educational funds.

**see discussion on rounding errors in Chapter 3.

Chapter 13

Church Custodians

Employment profile

Church custodians normally receive an hourly wage and function as church employees. Most are men, although women represent 45% of those working part-time. Some custodians are ordained ministers. The custodians surveyed provided the following employment profile:

Respondents:	Full-time	Part-time
❐ Number of Respondents	278	306
❐ Ordained	1%	1%
❐ Average Years Employed	8	6
❐ Male	84%	55%
❐ Female	16%	45%
❐ Self-employed	1%	11%
❐ Church Employee	99%	89%
❐ High School Diploma	81%	83%
❐ Associate's Degree	7%	5%
❐ Bachelor's Degree	10%	12%
❐ Master's Degree	2%	0%
❐ Doctorate	0%	0%

Compensation Analysis

The analysis below is based upon the tables found later in this chapter. The tables present compensation data according to worship attendance, church income, combinations of size and setting, gender, education, and years employed for church custodians who serve full-time. The final table provides data for part-time church custodians based upon the number of hours worked. In this way, the church custodian's compensation can be viewed from a variety of useful perspectives. The total compensation amount found in a separate box at the bottom of each page includes the base salary, housing or parsonage amount, life and health insurance payments, retirement contribution, and educational funds.

Key Points

✎ *Compensation increases gradually with church size.* The national average compensation corresponded to a church size of about 550 people. *See Table 13-1.*

✎ *The church's income was more of a predictor of compensation than was church size.* Compensation increased steadily with church income. The highest compensation levels occurred when churches had incomes over $1,000,000. *See Table 13-2.*

✎ *Urban and suburban churches provided the best income for churches with an average attendance below 500.* Yet in this group, all churches were below the national average. *See Table 13-3.*

✎ *More parity existed among churches with an average attendance above 500.* All congregations with an attendance above 500 provided compensation levels above the national average, except for those in small towns. *See Table 13-4.*

✎ *A significant difference existed in compensation levels between men and women.* On average, females earned 72% of their male counterparts. In general, men earned about $9,200 per year more than did women. Males worked in slightly smaller congregations, but with more income than the congregations in which the female custodians served. The differences are not enough to account for the disparity in compensation. *See Table 13-5.*

✎ *Most custodians are high school graduates.* About 12% were college graduates. In general, compensation increases for those with higher education. This is not always the case, however, and in some years, such as this one, those with a master's degree earn less than those with a high school education. *See Table 13-6.*

✎ *Compensation increased somewhat with years served.* While compensation increased with years served, this is not always the case. In some years, those serving on average thirteen years earn less than those who had worked on average eight years. Those with eight or less years of service earned below the national average. *See Table 13-7.*

✎ *On an hourly basis, part-time custodians earn less per hour than their full-time counterparts.* Most part-time custodians work about 17 hours per week. *See Table 13-8.*

Benefit Analysis

Full-time staff members. Church custodians received fewer and smaller benefits than full-time ministerial or professional staff. Over half received health insurance, but only 35% had any retirement program from the church. Benefits received were about the same as bookkeepers and more than secretaries.

Part-time church staff. About the same number of church custodians worked part-time as full-time. Fifty-two percent were part-time employees. Of this group, 45% were women. Eleven percent of the part-time custodians were self-employed. Churches provide part-time custodial workers very few benefits as compared to full-time employees. Part-time custodial work is primarily a straight hourly wage position.

Benefits	Full-time	Part-time
❒ Housing allowance	1%	1%
❒ Parsonage provided	1%	0%
❒ Retirement	35%	2%
❒ Life insurance	35%	2%
❒ Health insurance	63%	4%
❒ Paid vacation	88%	29%
❒ Auto allowance	75%	43%
❒ Continuing educational funds	6%	0%

Ten Year Compensation Trend: National Averages for Church Custodians

❒ 1996	$21,608
❒ 1997	$22,493
❒ 1998	$23,271
❒ 1999	$24,401
❒ 2000	$26,161
❒ 2001	$26,725
❒ 2002	$27,913
❒ 2003	$29,047
❒ 2004	$30,052
❒ 2005	$31,026

Table 13-1: Annual Compensation of Custodian by Worship Attendance

Church Attendance	0-99	100-299	300-499	500-749	750-999	over 1000
Number Of Respondents	0	45	64	57	34	71
Salary (99%*)		20,884	23,538	27,067	28,635	30,624
Annual % Increase (76%*)		3%	3%	3%	3%	4%
Parsonage (1%)		12,000	6,622	0	0	5,400
Housing (1%)		0	23,831	3,600	14,400	0
Retirement (35%)		1,243	1,988	2,021	1,801	1,773
Life Insurance (35%)		182	399	235	725	189
Health Insurance (63%)		6,136	5,053	5,680	6,346	6,126
Vacation/weeks (88%)		3	3	3	3	3
Education Fund (6%)		150	300	826	500	1,185
Auto Allowance (75%)		60%	66%	79%	85%	86%

* The percentage following each compensation item indicates the portion of custodians who received that form of compensation. The averages in each column are for those individuals who actually received that compensation item. See Chapter 3 for a full explanation of how to read this table.

Total Compensation Comparisons At A Glance

Worship Attendance	0-99	100-299	300-499	500-749	750-999	over 1,000
Average attendance		201	385	596	848	1,638
Average church income		549,244	908,026	1,395,497	1,818,381	3,062,886
Average years employed		7	8	8	8	8
Average compensation*		23,857	27,381	32,056	34,162	36,100
Standard deviation		7,531	8,851	12,013	12,241	11,756
Median compensation		22,752	28,000	30,739	31,000	35,205

National average: $31,026 with a standard deviation of $11,695 (see Chapter 4, Table 4-3)

Total respondents: 271

* includes base salary, housing or parsonage allowance, retirement contributions, life and health insurance payments, and educational funds.

Table 13-2: Annual Compensation of Custodian by Church Budget

Church Budget in $	0-249,999	250,000-499,999	500,000-749,000	750,000-999,999	1,000,000 +
Number Of Respondents	7	23	37	35	159
Salary (99%*)	19,328	20,178	22,831	25,917	28,435
Annual % Increase (76%)	4%	3%	3%	3%	4%
Parsonage (1%)	12,000	0	0	0	8,807
Housing (1%)	0	0	0	0	13,716
Retirement (35%)	4,152	1,198	1,635	2,041	1,863
Life Insurance (35%)	120	159	126	250	322
Health Insurance (63%)	6,864	6,541	5,462	5,702	5,859
Vacation/weeks (88%)	2	3	3	3	3
Education Fund (6%)	0	150	100	300	829
Auto Allowance (75%)	71%	61%	59%	63%	82%

* The percentage following each compensation item indicates the portion of custodians who received that form of compensation. The averages in each column are for those individuals who actually received that compensation item. See Chapter 3 for a full explanation of how to read this table.

Total Compensation Comparisons

Church Budget	0-249,000	250,000-499,999	500,000-749,999	750,000-999,999	1,000,000+
Average attendance	148	205	392	395	1,042
Average church income	200,021	374,932	625,508	869,586	2,274,829
Average years employed	10	6	8	9	8
Average compensation*	23,672	22,172	25,824	29,799	33,909
Standard deviation	8,881	7,672	9,806	7,150	11,738
Median compensation	16,551	21,580	24,000	29,358	32,500

National average: $31,026 with a standard deviation of $11,695 (see Chapter 4, Table 4-3)

Total respondents: 261

* includes base salary, housing or parsonage allowance, retirement contributions, life and health insurance payments, and educational funds.

Table 13-3: Annual Compensation of Custodian by Church Setting And Size

Attendance Under 500	Urban	Suburban	Medium City	Small Town	Rural
Number Of Respondents	17	29	34	28	0
Salary (99%*)	22,829	24,620	22,300	19,759	
Annual % Increase (76%)	4%	3%	4%	3%	
Parsonage (1%)	6,622	12,000	0	0	
Housing (1%)	23,831	0	0	0	
Retirement (35%)	2,142	1,727	1,457	1,565	
Life Insurance (35%)	209	649	290	256	
Health Insurance (63%)	5,479	5,386	5,437	5,435	
Vacation/weeks (88%)	3	3	3	2	
Education Fund (6%)	300	0	150	0	
Auto Allowance (75%)	88%	59%	53%	61%	

* The percentage following each compensation item indicates the portion of custodians who received that form of compensation. The averages in each column are for those individuals who actually received that compensation item. See Chapter 3 for a full explanation of how to read this table.

Total Compensation Comparisons

Attendance Under 500	Urban	Suburban	Medium City	Small Town	Rural
Average attendance	294	308	297	315	
Average church income	870,178	660,220	774,396	722,043	
Average years employed	6	10	8	6	
Average compensation*	28,672	27,962	25,888	22,119	
Standard deviation	7,853	6,702	7,524	9,964	
Median compensation	24,957	27,965	24,475	21,195	

National average: $31,026 with a standard deviation of $11,695 (see Chapter 4, Table 4-3)

Total respondents: 108

* includes base salary, housing or parsonage allowance, retirement contributions, life and health insurance payments, and educational funds.

Table 13-4: Annual Compensation of Custodian by Church Setting And Size

Attendance Over 499	Urban	Suburban	Medium City	Small Town	Rural
Number Of Respondents	26	65	50	16	3
Salary (99%*)	30,522	29,228	29,463	23,548	30,758
Annual % Increase (76%)	4%	4%	3%	4%	4%
Parsonage (1%)	0	14,400	5,400	0	0
Housing (1%)	0	0	3,600	0	0
Retirement (35%)	2,305	1,961	1,760	1,129	855
Life Insurance (35%)	338	377	185	93	166
Health Insurance (63%)	6,067	6,260	5,844	6,480	3,688
Vacation/weeks (88%)	3	3	3	3	3
Education Fund (6%)	250	301	820	0	775
Auto Allowance (75%)	81%	82%	90%	75%	67%

* The percentage following each compensation item indicates the portion of custodians who received that form of compensation. The averages in each column are for those individuals who actually received that compensation item. See Chapter 3 for a full explanation of how to read this table.

Total Compensation Comparisons

Attendance Over 499	Urban	Suburban	Medium City	Small Town	Rural
Average attendance	1,059	1,216	1,109	768	1,115
Average church income	2,490,970	2,527,131	2,022,969	1,519,998	1,817,639
Average years employed	11	8	7	9	5
Average compensation*	36,408	34,904	35,136	28,057	34,100
Standard deviation	12,188	12,997	9,637	11,042	14,200
Median compensation	33,800	32,500	34,008	27,004	35,430

National average: $31,026 with a standard deviation of $11,695 (see Chapter 4, Table 4-3)

Total respondents: 160

* includes base salary, housing or parsonage allowance, retirement contributions, life and health insurance payments, and educational funds.

Table 13-5: Annual Compensation of Custodian by Gender

Gender	Male	Female
Number Of Respondents	229	44
Salary (99%*)	27,689	20,161
Annual % Increase (76%)	4%	3%
Parsonage (1%)	9,606	0
Housing (1%)	23,831	0
Retirement (35%)	1,921	1,502
Life Insurance (35%)	321	165
Health Insurance (63%)	5,806	5,785
Vacation/weeks (88%)	3	2
Education Fund (6%)	995	51
Auto Allowance (75%)	75%	80%

* The percentage following each compensation item indicates the portion of custodians who received that form of compensation. The averages in each column are for those individuals who actually received that compensation item. See Chapter 3 for a full explanation of how to read this table.

Total Compensation Comparisons

Gender	Male	Female
Average attendance	773	840
Average church income	1,664,069	1,497,675
Average years employed	8	7
Average compensation*	32,523	23,311
Standard deviation	11,786	8,276
Median compensation	31,919	22,162

National average: $31,026 with a standard deviation of $11,695 (see Chapter 4, Table 4-3)

Total respondents: 273

* includes base salary, housing or parsonage allowance, retirement contributions, life and health insurance payments, and educational funds.

Table 13-6: Annual Compensation of Custodian by Education

Highest Degree	High School	Associate	Bachelor	Master	Doctorate
Number Of Respondents	150	12	19	3	
Salary (99%*)	26,180	30,819	29,223	24,850	
Annual % Increase (76%)	3%	4%	3%	3%	
Parsonage (1%)	9,311	0	0	0	
Housing (1%)	0	0	23,831	0	
Retirement (35%)	1,869	1,681	1,263	840	
Life Insurance (35%)	312	310	233	0	
Health Insurance (63%)	6,262	5,200	5,908	3,320	
Vacation/weeks (88%)	3	3	2	3	
Education Fund (6%)	1,619	713	500	0	
Auto Allowance (75%)	77%	100%	68%	67%	

* The percentage following each compensation item indicates the portion of custodians who received that form of compensation. The averages in each column are for those individuals who actually received that compensation item. See Chapter 3 for a full explanation of how to read this table.

Total Compensation Comparisons

Highest Degree	High School	Associate	Bachelor	Master	Doctorate
Average attendance	799	987	737	967	
Average church income	1,730,835	1,824,100	1,191,540	1,265,820	
Average years employed	8	6	7	17	
Average compensation*	31,034	35,404	34,031	27,343	
Standard deviation	11,932	14,799	11,634	11,077	
Median compensation	29,622	36,593	29,094	33,046	

National average: $31,026 with a standard deviation of $11,695 (see Chapter 4, Table 4-3)

Total respondents: 184

* includes base salary, housing or parsonage allowance, retirement contributions, life and health insurance payments, and educational funds.

Table 13-7: Annual Compensation of Custodian by Years Employed

Years Employed	0-5	6-10	11-15	over 15
Number Of Respondents	138	63	36	34
Salary (99%*)	24,707	25,778	28,809	30,690
Annual % Increase (76%)	4%	3%	3%	3%
Parsonage (1%)	14,400	6,011	0	12,000
Housing (1%)	13,716	0	0	0
Retirement (35%)	1,537	1,585	2,210	2,765
Life Insurance (35%)	419	152	206	350
Health Insurance (63%)	5,588	5,601	6,419	6,141
Vacation/weeks (88%)	2	3	3	4
Education Fund (6%)	1,013	350	200	401
Auto Allowance (75%)	77%	78%	78%	68%

* The percentage following each compensation item indicates the portion of custodians who received that form of compensation. The averages in each column are for those individuals who actually received that compensation item. See Chapter 3 for a full explanation of how to read this table.

Total Compensation Comparisons

Years Employed	0-5	6-10	11-15	over 15
Average attendance	732	920	772	710
Average church income	1,447,121	1,934,025	1,533,246	1,950,299
Average years employed	3	8	13	23
Average compensation*	28,980	30,449	33,449	36,385
Standard deviation	11,697	10,718	12,161	10,583
Median compensation	28,071	28,300	31,919	34,600

National average: $31,026 with a standard deviation of $11,695 (see Chapter 4, Table 4-3)

Total respondents: 271

* includes base salary, housing or parsonage allowance, retirement contributions, life and health insurance payments, and educational funds.

Table 13-8: Annual Compensation of Part-Time Custodians by Hours Worked

Hours-per-week	1-14	15-29	30-39	All Part-time
Number Of Respondents	53	69	23	306
Salary (97%*)	6,684	10,733	15,214	9,257
Annual % Increase (45%)	4%	4%	4%	4%
Parsonage (0%)	0	0	0	0
Housing (1%)	0	0	0	11,100
Retirement (2%)	0	900	1,196	1,280
Life Insurance (2%)	0	56	264	168
Health Insurance (4%)	0	0	7,291	7,526
Vacation/weeks (29%)	2	2	3	2
Education Funds (0%)	0	0	0	0
Auto Allowance (43%)	43%	59%	61%	43%

* The percentage following each compensation item indicates the portion of part-timecustodians who received that form of compensation. The averages in each column are for those individuals who actually received that compensation item. See Chapter 3 for a full explanation of how to read this table.

Total Compensation Comparisons

Hours Worked Per Week	1-14	15-29	30-39	All Part-time
Average attendance	189	384	409	292
Average church income	306,866	685,273	787,372	507,549
Average years employed	5	7	6	6
Average hours per week	8	20	31	17
Average compensation	6,684	10,748	16,914	9,597
Ave. hourly compensation*	16.07	10.33	10.49	10.86
Average hourly salary**	16.07	10.32	9.44	10.47

Total respondents: 306

* includes base salary, housing or parsonage allowance, retirement contributions, life and health insurance payments, and educational funds. See discussion on "rounding errors" in Chapter 3.

Chapter 14

Statistical Abstract of Participating Churches

In addition to the individual compensation surveys, many of the participating churches also completed a congregational profile. That information is presented below. Data is presented according to Sunday worship attendance. Five size categories are portrayed. Second, attendance and income trends are presented according to both church *size* and *setting*.

Key Findings

☐ Congregations with a Sunday morning worship attendance between 501-750 experienced the highest per capita giving.

☐ On average, 47% of the church budget is devoted to salaries.

☐ About 37% of churches provide additional salary to their ordained staff members to assist them with their social security payments. Of those churches that do help, 40% pay one-half of the social security tax while 34% pay all of it.

☐ Eighty-seven percent of the participating churches reimburse the professional expenses of their ordained employees. The average reimbursement was $3,287, almost identical to last year, but down from $3,534 two years ago, and $3,774 three years ago.

☐ The majority of churches (94%) require a full accounting of professional expenses including date, purpose, location, and amount of expense before a reimbursement is made.

☐ A high percentage (96%) of churches in our sample were connected to the Internet. This was up from 94% last year and up from just 83% four years ago. The likelihood of being connected increases with church size.

☐ For the second consecutive year, a majority of congregations did not experience an increase in church attendance over the past three years. However, a majority of congregations with an attendance over 750 reported growth. Prior to 2004, there had been over a decade on consistent growth.

☐ Forty-five percent of the participating churches reported that their income exceeded expenses during the past year, up from 41% last year. This is the first increase in three years. Four years ago it was 58%, three years ago it was 55%, and last year it was 41%.

Congregational Profile By Church Worship Attendance

	All n=901	0-250 n=438	251-500 n=219	501-750 n=92	751-1000 n=54	over 1000 n=82
Worship Attendance	432	129	369	629	890	1,702
Total income	$840,340	$260,416	$730,787	$1,342,442	$1,847,188	$2,980,940
Per capita: attendance	$1,945	$2,019	$1,980	$2,134	$2,075	$1,751
What percentage is compensation of your total church budget?	47%	46%	48%	49%	47%	48%
Number of Ordained Staff Full-time/Part-time	3/2	1/1	3/1	3/1	4/2	7/2
Number of Nonordained Staff Full-time/Part-time	6.6/	2/3	3/5	6/8	7/13	18/16
Contributes to social security payments of ordained staff	37%	33%	44%	36%	31%	34%
Pays all	34%	22%	19%	18%	17%	0%
Pays half	40%	40%	36%	24%	17%	29%
Reimburses professional expenses (average amount reimbursed)	87% $3,287	85% $2,928	91% $3,215	88% $3,503	86% $3,150	85% $5,053
Requires a full accounting including date, purpose, location and amount before reimbursing expenses	94%	93%	92%	96%	100%	95%
Church has a connection to the Internet	96%	92%	100%	100%	100%	100%
Individual completing questionnaire has a connection to the Internet at home	95%	93%	94%	98%	100%	100%

Attendance and Income Trends by Church Size

Attendance Trend Over the Past Three Years	Decline	Stable	Increase
All Churches (901)	15%	40%	45%
0-250 (438)	20%	40%	40%
251-500 (219)	11%	43%	46%
501-750 (92)	12%	47%	41%
751-1000 (54)	8%	22%	70%
over 1000 (82)	12%	26%	62%

Financial Status	Income below expenses	Income meets expenses	Income above expenses
All churches (901)	17%	38%	45%
0-250 (438)	21%	40%	39%
251-500 (219)	16%	42%	42%
501-750 (92)	16%	37%	47%
751-1000 (54)	12%	33%	55%
over 1000 (82)	8%	24%	68%

Attendance and Income Trends by Geographical Setting

Attendance Trend Over the Past Three Years	Decline	Stable	Increase
All Churches (901)	15%	40%	45%
Urban (104)	24%	44%	33%
Suburban (291)	15%	39%	46%
Medium Size City (203)	15%	35%	50%
Small Town (214)	12%	44%	44%
Rural (76)	13%	38%	49%

Financial Status	Income below expenses	Income meets expenses	Income above expenses
All Churches (901)	17%	38%	45%
Urban (108)	30%	37%	33%
Suburban (291)	16%	37%	47%
Medium Size City (203)	18%	37%	45%
Small Town (214)	10%	41%	49%
Rural (76)	15%	36%	49%

Appendix 1

Ten Year Compensation Trend

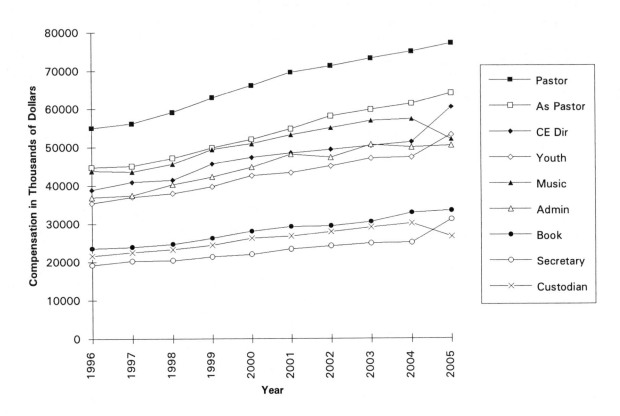

Appendix 2

Compensation and Church Income

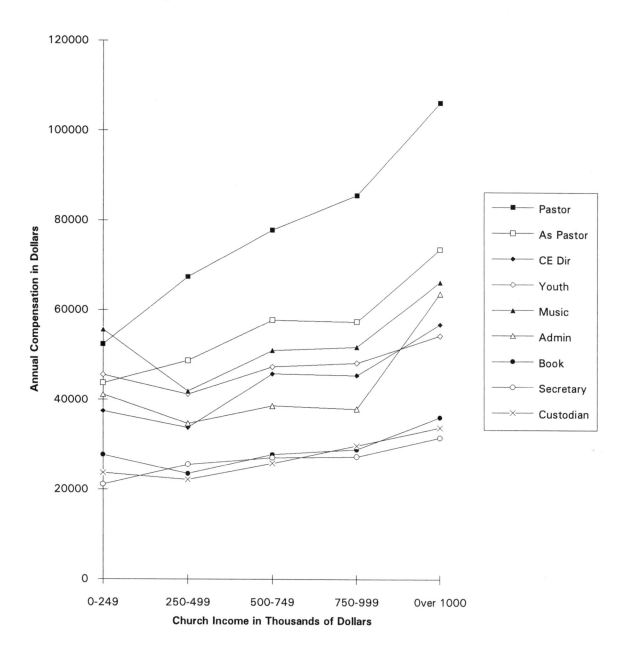

Appendix 3

Compensation and Church Attendance

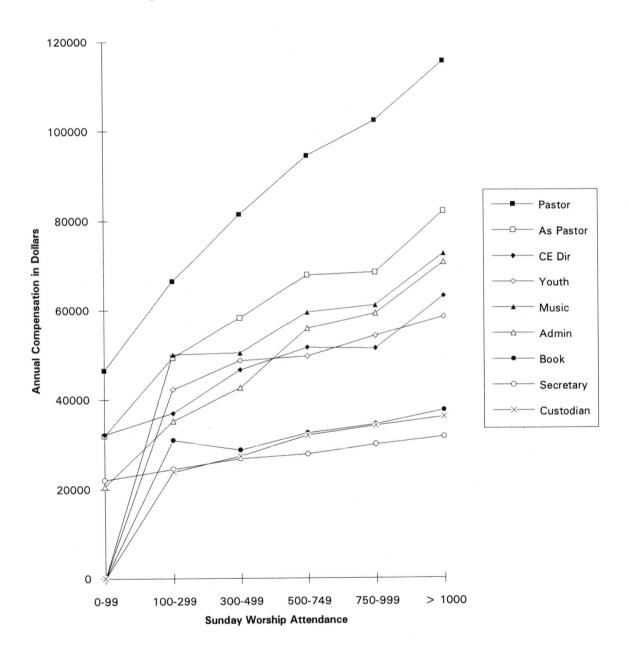

Appendix 4

Compensation Averages by Education

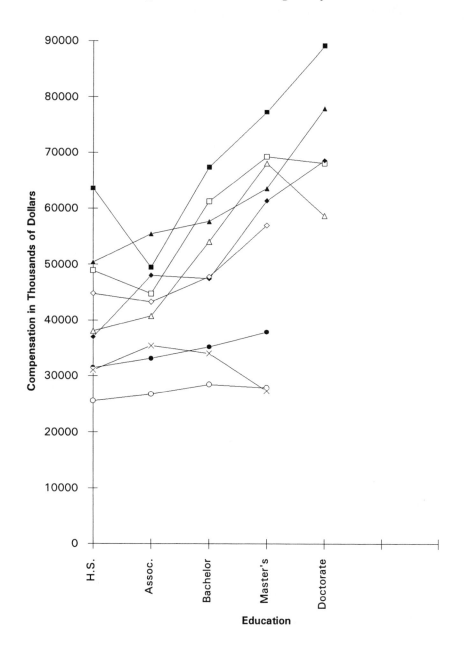

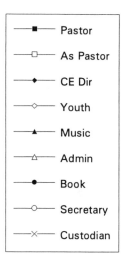

112360

Appendix 5

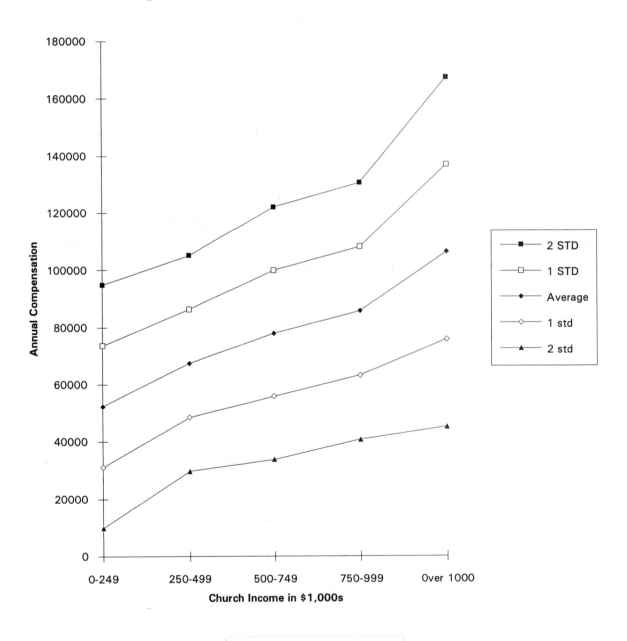

Standard Deviation Ranges for Pastoral Compensation Based on Church Income